STUDIES IN ISAIAH XL–LXVI

STUDIES IN ISAIAH XL–LXVI

WITH AN INTRODUCTORY CHAPTER
ON THE COMPOSITE CHARACTER OF
ISAIAH I–XXXIX

By the Rev.
W. O. E. OESTERLEY, D.D

Examining Chaplain to the Bishop of London;
Warburton Lecturer in Lincoln's Inn,
Vicar of St Alban's, Bedford Park, W

Author of
"*THE BOOKS OF THE APOCRYPHA   Their Origin, Teaching and Contents*"

WIPF & STOCK · Eugene, Oregon

Wipf and Stock Publishers
199 W 8th Ave, Suite 3
Eugene, OR 97401

Studies in Isaiah XL-LXVI
With an Introductory Chapter on
the Composite Character of Isaiah I-XXXIX
By Oesterley, W. O. E.
Softcover ISBN-13: 978-1-6667-3425-6
Hardcover ISBN-13: 978-1-6667-2991-7
eBook ISBN-13: 978-1-6667-2992-4
Publication date 8/19/2021
Previously published by Robert Scott, 1916

This edition is a scanned facsimile of
the original edition published in 1916.

PREFATORY NOTE

THE following Studies form the elaboration of a course of lectures given in Cambridge last year to the students who came up for the *Vacation Term for Biblical Study*. The Studies have, with three exceptions, been selected with the object of dealing with such subjects as, from their nature, cannot be discussed at much length in Commentaries; this applies more especially to the doctrinal and archæological Studies, which take up the major part of the following pages. Points of exegesis can also be dealt with more at length in a lecture than in a commentary where the entire text of a book has to be explained. The two first Studies, which are introductory, deal with the composite character of the book of Isaiah; this, though amply considered in the Commentaries, seemed to be a necessary preliminary here too, because it has a direct bearing on the different doctrinal standpoints in the book. A brief historical survey was also considered appropriate as the historical background of the book has so much to do with the proper understanding of it. It has not been thought necessary to give a list of books on *Isaiah*, especially as commentaries have not been made much use of ; light on the various passages discussed has been sought in many diverse quarters, the enumeration of which would not be possible ; for in reading one absorbs some things from others, and some are evolved out of one's own mind ; and later on it becomes difficult to ascertain the origin of some of the things that are written down.

W. O. E. OESTERLEY.

St Alban's Vicarage,
Bedford Park, W.
January, 1916.

CONTENTS

	PAGE
PREFATORY NOTE	v

I THE COMPOSITE CHARACTER OF THE BOOK
    OF ISAIAH 3
    (1) *Isaianic and non-Isaianic elements* . 5
    (2) *Redactional additions to the text, and
        their objects* 11

II THE COMPONENT PARTS OF ISAIAH xl.–
    lxvi., THEIR CONTENTS AND DATE . 25
    (1) *Chapters xl –lv* 27
    (2) *The Ebed-Jahwe Songs* . . . 31
    (3) *Chapters lvi –lxvi.* 43

III A BRIEF SURVEY OF THE HISTORICAL
    BACKGROUND OF ISAIAH xl –lxvi. . 49
    (1) *Judæa after the Fall of Jerusalem
        and during the Captivity* . . 50
    (2) *The Exiles in Babylon* . . . 54
    (3) *The Jews in Palestine after the Re-
        turn* 58

IV THE DOCTRINAL STANDPOINT OF ISAIAH
    xl.–lv. 67
    (1) *The Doctrine of Atonement* . . 69
    (2) *The Doctrine of God* . . . 74

V THE DOCTRINAL STANDPOINT OF THE EBED-
    JAHWE SONGS 85

CONTENTS

		PAGE
VI	THE DOCTRINAL STANDPOINT OF ISAIAH lvi.–lxvi.	107
	(1) *The Observance of the Law*	111
	(2) *The Observance of the Sabbath*	113
	(3) *Almsgiving*	117
	(4) *Superhuman Beings*	121
VII	EXEGETICAL STUDIES	133
	xl 3	134
	xl 22	136
	xliv 3	137
	xliv 6	138
	xliv 8	140
	l 10, 11	143
	li 6	145
	li. 9–11	149
	lvi 4, 5	151
	lvii. 1, 2	153
VIII	ARCHÆOLOGICAL AND OTHER STUDIES	157
	xliv. 5	157
	xlvii 13	163
	lvi. 4, 5	164
	lvii. 3–9	166
	lxv–5, lxvi. 17	170
	INDEX	181

I

THE COMPOSITE CHARACTER OF THE BOOK OF ISAIAH

STUDIES IN ISAIAH XL—LXVI

I

THE COMPOSITE CHARACTER OF THE BOOK OF ISAIAH

THE time is past, it may be hoped, in which exception can be taken to the contention that a book of the Bible contains writings from the hand of more than one author. Not merely specialists in biblical study but also the ordinary student of the Bible recognizes nowadays that it is not a spirit of wanton, destructive criticism which compels the discriminating scholar to differ from many of the traditional views regarding the authorship of biblical books. The evidence of those books themselves is too strong to be ignored. To take, as an example, the book of Isaiah: the historical references contained here show that the period covered dates from about 740 B.C. to about 540 B.C. at least. If the whole of this book is to be regarded as having been written by the prophet Isaiah we should either have to suppose that he lived for well over 200 years, or else that he foresaw the events which were going to happen, not only among his own people, but also among foreign nation s a good hundred years (at the least) before they came to pass. Both suppositions are altogether unnatural. And there is another difficulty which is not less serious, namely, the difference in the religious standpoint between the two main divisions of the book, not to mention any other divisions. It is impossible to account satisfactorily for these differences on any supposition other than that the authors of the two parts respectively lived in different ages in the second of which a fundamental change had taken place in the national religion. To enter into the details of this change is not our present purpose, but some idea of their far-reaching character will be gained as we proceed.

But it is not sufficient to recognize difference of authorship in the two main divisions of the book of Isaiah ; the arguments upon which this is based apply also when each of these main divisions is individually examined. It is not our intention to deal otherwise than cursorily with this subject so far as Isaiah i.–

COMPOSITE CHARACTER OF BOOK 5

xxxix. is concerned, though a few sentences must be devoted to show that this division is not homogeneous. Isaiah xl.–lxvi. will receive fuller treatment.

(1) *Isaianic and non-Isaianic Elements.*

Allowing for certain redactional elements of which a word will be said presently, the following chapters are recognized by the majority of scholars to be Isaianic in the main : i.–xii., xiv. 24–32, xv.–xviii., xxii., xxiii., xxviii.–xxxiii. With these we need not deal since our purpose in this section is merely to show that the book of Isaiah is of composite authorship. It will be well, however, to indicate briefly why the remainder of the chapters in this division of the book are not to be regarded as the work of Isaiah.

xiii. 1–*xiv.* 23. The historical background of this section, which consists of a prophecy (xiii. 1–22) and a song of triumph (xiv. 1–23), is the same as that of the opening chapters of the second part of Isaiah, namely the Exile, which is however drawing near to its close, for the downfall of Babylon is imminent. This is clear from xiii. 17 : *Behold, I will stir up the Medes against them*, i.e. the people of Babylon; and from xiii. 19—

And Babylon, the glory of kingdoms,
The beauty of the Chaldeans' pride,
Shall be as when God overthrew
Sodom and Gomorrah (cp. xiv. 22).

Moreover, the whole song of triumph is in celebration of Israel's delivery from captivity which is about to be accomplished, e.g. xiv. 3, 4: *And it shall come to pass in the day that the Lord shall give thee rest from thy sorrow, and from thy trouble, and from the hard service wherein thou wast made to serve, that thou shalt take up this parable against the king of Babylon, and say, How hath the oppressor ceased.* . . . This all points to a time long subsequent to that of Isaiah. "It is the office of the prophet of Israel to address himself to the needs of his own age, to announce to his contemporaries the judgements, or consolations, which arose out of the circumstances of their own time, to interpret for them their own history. To base a promise upon a condition of things *not yet existent*, and without any point of contact with the circumstances or situation of those to whom

COMPOSITE CHARACTER OF BOOK 7

it is addressed, is alien to the genius of prophecy."[1]

xix. This chapter has always been recognized by commentators as one of peculiar difficulty. One thing, however, seems clear; it consists of two compositions, vv. 1–15 and vv. 16–25. The former of these is in many respects reminiscent of Isaiah, and as it is a prophecy against Egypt, not a few scholars regard it as having been uttered by Isaiah who was contemplating an Assyrian invasion of Egypt. It is possible that within the lifetime of Isaiah five such invasions either took place or might have been expected. The Egyptians were twice defeated by Sargon, in 720 and 711; once by Sennacherib in 701; Egypt was actually invaded by Esarhaddon about the year 672 and was reduced to the position of an Assyrian province; and again in about 660 a Libyan invasion took place unde Psammetichus who subjugated the land. There are therefore, *historically*, ample grounds for assigning xix. 1–15 to Isaiah; nevertheless, there is such a marked difference in style and diction between this prophecy and

[1] Driver, *Introduction to the Literature of the Old Testament*, p. 201.

those universally acknowledged to be the work of Isaiah that there is a real difficulty in believing that this piece could have been written by him. The similarities with Isaianic authorship which xix. 1–15 contains are easily and naturally accounted for on the assumption that they are imitations, probably unconscious, on the part of disciples of the prophet. As to the second part of this section, verses 16–25, Box rightly points out that " it manifests a broad universalism—contemplating the fusion of Israelites and non-Israelites—which is hardly conceivable before the Greek period (subsequent to Alexander the Great). Indeed in verse 18 there seems to be an explicit reference to Jewish colonists in Egypt who still spoke *the language of Canaan.*" [1]

xx. The fact that Isaiah is here spoken of in the third person, and that the passage contains a reference to that prophet's symbolic act of walking *naked and barefoot three years for a sign and a wonder upon Egypt and upon Ethiopia*, is presumptive evidence, at least, against Isaianic authorship. That it belongs to the time of Isaiah is probable enough.

[1] *The Book of Isaiah*, p. 92.

xxi. This chapter consists of three oracles entirely independent of each other. There is diversity of opinion as to whether these three pieces are to be regarded as belonging to the prophet Isaiah; but of one thing there can be no doubt, especially to the Hebrew scholar, viz. the style of writing characteristic of all three, a style which is "peculiarly obscure and enigmatic."[1] In comparing them with the undoubted writings of Isaiah it is difficult to believe that they can have come from his hand.

xxiv.–xxvii. There is a consensus of opinion among scholars that these chapters do not belong to Isaiah. Their apocalyptic character points to a much later age. Other considerations likewise point to the improbability of their having been written by Isaiah. As Driver truly says, "The style is more artificial than that of Isaiah, as appears, for instance, in the frequent combination of nearly synonymous clauses, the repetition of a word, the numerous alliterations and word-plays, the tendency to rhyme—all features which, though they may be found occasionally in Isaiah, are never aggregated in his writings as they are

[1] Box, *Op cit*, p 96

here. There are, moreover, many unusual expressions, the *combination* of which points similarly to an author other than Isaiah."[1] There are undoubtedly various points of contact in the section, " but in the light of the general difference these are not sufficient to establish Isaiah's authorship ; they do not show more than that the author was familiar with Isaiah's writings, and sometimes borrowed expressions from them."[2]

xxxiv., xxxv. What was said regarding xxiv.–xxvii. applies in part here ; the eschatological character of these chapters belongs to a later age than that of Isaiah, and their literary style is not Isaiah's.

xxxvi.–xxxix. These chapters are extracts, with small and unimportant variations, from 2 Kings xviii., xix, to which was added the Song of Hezekiah (Is. xxxviii. 9–20).

These, then, are the non-Isaianic portions in Isaiah i.–xxix., and the reasons, put in the briefest possible way, for regarding them as non-Isaianic. It is well to realize this composite character of the first great division of the book of Isaiah, for we shall find that the case is not otherwise in the second great division,

[1] Driver, *Op. cit.*, p. 209.   [2] *Ibid.*

though in this latter there is not so much diversity of authorship. But both divisions partake of a further characteristic noticeable throughout, we refer to redactional modifications and additions. There is by no means always certainty as to where and to what extent the redactor has been active, and it is possible that some commentators have been over-zealous in seeking for the traces of his handiwork; but that the whole book of Isaiah, as we now have it, has been subjected to considerable modifications owing to the work of one or more redactors cannot be gainsaid by any serious student of the book.

(2) *Redactional additions to the text, and their object.*

A word may be said, in passing, as to the object of these redactional additions, and the reasons owing to which commentators have been led to believe that a passage is not an original part of the text. The few illustrations which will be given here are taken from the first division of the book (Isa. i.–xxxix.) only, though the reasons for their having been made apply, on general grounds, to the rest of the book, and indeed more or less to the books of the Old Testament as a whole. Our first example is ii. 5 : *O house of Jacob, come ye and let us walk in the light of Jahwe.* The preceding section (ii. 2–4, cp. Mic. iv. 1–3) is a self-contained eschatological poem of three divisions or " verses," each with six nearly equal lines ; neither in form nor contents has verse 5 any connexion with it. The section which follows it (verses 6–8) is again, as its contents clearly show, another independent poem ; its rhythm is also different from that of verses 2–4 ; and again verse 5 has no connexion with it. The critical reader, seeing this verse standing by itself and having nothing to do either with what precedes or follows, naturally concludes that it did not stand there originally ; a conclusion which is strengthened when it is realized that " to walk in the light of Jahwe " means to walk in His Law,[1] an idea which belongs to later times. Why, then, was it added ? In all probability for this reason : if one reads the text as it stood originally (i.e. without verse 5) there are, as we have seen, two independent poems joined together though differing in both form and subject-matter ; and yet the second of these

---

[1] Cp Prov. vi. 23 : *The commandment is a lamp ; and the law is light ;* the book of Proverbs is admittedly a late book ; cp also the late Psalm cxix. 105 *Thy word is a lamp unto my feet, and a light unto my path.*

COMPOSITE CHARACTER OF BOOK 13

begins with : "*For* thou hast forsaken . . ." as though it were closely connected with what precedes. An editor, seeing the incongruity of this, desired to put in something which would act as a kind of link to join the two together in some sort of way, and knowing his Bible well (as those old scribes always did) he looked up the parallel passage of Isaiah ii. 2-4 in Micah (iv. 1-3), and saw that in close connexion with the passage there stood the words : "We will walk in the name of Jahwe our God for ever"; this he adapted, being zealous for the Law, and made out of it an exhortation to walk according to the Law, i.e. the light of Jahwe. It was not altogether a successful link, but it smoothed over to some extent the incongruity he found; an incongruity which had arisen in earlier days through piecing together prophecies and fragments of prophecies which were in reality wholly independent.

Our next example is that of an addition which is found within verses 9-11 of chapter xxii. If we were to read the text of these verses in this way :

And ye looked [1] (*in that day*) *to the armour of the house of the forest,*

[1] The Hebrew reads now "thou didst look"; but as

*And ye saw the breaches of the city of David,
    that they were many;
But ye looked not unto Him that did this,
Ye beheld not Him who pre-ordained it long
    since.*

There is a smoothness in style and thought here which is perfect; the prophet is upbraiding the people for trusting to themselves in the day of stress rather than to God; they looked to their armour, they looked to the breaches in the walls of Jerusalem, i.e. they restored them; but they never thought of God in whose foreknowledge are all things. Now when we turn to the text we find that after the words "that they were many," there is inserted, not in rhythmic measure like the rest of the text, but in prose, this that follows: "And ye gathered together the waters of the lower pool, and ye broke down the houses to fortify the wall; ye made also a reservoir between the two walls for the water of the old pool." One can see at once that this insertion spoils the symmetry and the strophic balance of the

all the other verbs are in the plural, and as a slight change would make this verb also the plural, it is evident that a textual error has crept in and that we ought to read "ye looked."

COMPOSITE CHARACTER OF BOOK 15

text, besides being quite unnecessary. Isaiah does not go into prosaic details such as this insertion contains, it is not his way; great truths and principles are what fill his mind. For these reasons practically all modern commentators regard the prose passage as not belonging to the original words of Isaiah; and one cannot but feel that they are right. The object that a redactor in later times had in view when he added the insertion was to amplify what the prophet had said. The prophet was referring to what we read of in 2 Kings xx. 20; 2 Chronicles xxxii. 5; the redactor, seeing that there were several details to which the prophet did not refer, thought well to add these from 2 Chronicles xxxii. 3, 4.

An example of a different character, but one to which it is well to call attention as it is of a kind that often occurs in the Old Testament, is a small addition to the second line of xxx. 26; the first two lines of this verse run thus:

And the light of the moon shall be as the light of the sun,
And the light of the sun shall be sevenfold.

To this someone has added: " Like the

light of seven days." The addition is, on the face of it, unnecessary; it spoils the rhythm of the text, and, what is also important, it does not occur in the Septuagint; which shows that the addition must be a very late one. Glosses of this kind which were, in all probability, stray thoughts jotted down as marginal notes and ultimately incorporated into the text, are of frequent occurrence in the Old Testament.

One more example must suffice. We get a logical and straightforward passage if we read xxxiii. 22, 23*b*, 24 together, thus:

> *For Jahwe is our Judge,*
> *Jahwe is our Lawgiver,*
> *Jahwe is our King;*
> *He will save us.*
> *Then shall the blind divide great spoil,* (amended text)
> *The lame (too) shall take the booty;*
> *No inhabitant shall say, " I am sick,"*
> *The people that dwell therein, their iniquity shall be forgiven.*

The words of the text as it stands here tell of the reward that follows when the people take God for their Judge, and Lawgiver, and King; even the blind and lame come off well; and there is forgiveness of sin for all.

COMPOSITE CHARACTER OF BOOK

Now in the Hebrew text as it now stands there occurs after the words, "He will save us," this passage:

> *Thy tacklings are loosed,*
> *The foot of their mast they hold not,*
> *They spread not out the sail.*

Nobody can fail to see how utterly incongruous these words are here; it is quite impossible to believe that they formed part of the text originally. Why, then, were they added? That is difficult to say; we can only offer a tentative reply. Conceivably the reason may be this: the preceding verses depict the glory of Jerusalem that shall be her's in the Messianic times, when there shall be peace and safety for the people; and the prophet, in a picture, conceives of the land transformed, and he sees in his mind's eye a broad stream, so grateful in a dry country, flowing through the land, whereon are no ships or fleet, for all shall be peaceful and calm; he expresses this in verse 21, the Hebrew text is somewhat corrupt, and the following translation is based on an amended text:

> *But there shall be for us a mighty river,*
> *A place of broad rivers and streams,*

*No fleet with oars shall go thereon,
No gallant ship shall sail there.*

In later days as a scribe was reading and pondering over this he recalled what he had read about the great ships of Tarshish in Ezekiel xxvii. 25 ff., where that prophet had uttered his lamentation over Tyre; how these ships had been wrecked and gone down into the depth of the sea; and how the once proud Tyre had been brought to degradation and ruin. He is struck by the great contrast between the picture of Jerusalem's future glory given by the prophet he is reading and Ezekiel's picture of the downfall of Tyre; and he gives expression to his thoughts by writing on the margin a fragment reminiscent of fallen Tyre who had put all her trust in her wonderful ships. Then, later on, when other scribes came to make further copies of the Scriptures, that reader's fragment, instead of being regarded as a passing comment, was added as part of the text.

This is, of course, all supposition; but it is conceivable that in some such ways many passages have found their way into the text of the Old Testament whose presence there is otherwise not easy to account for.

COMPOSITE CHARACTER OF BOOK 19

These illustrations have taken us somewhat far afield; but it has perhaps been worth while giving them, for though they have been taken only from the first half of the book of Isaiah, what has been said regarding them applies equally to many additions found in Isaiah xl.-lxvi. These illustrations only present a few of the objects for which redactional additions have been made, but the following list summarizes those objects. Space forbids us to give examples, so we must content ourselves with merely stating the objects. Redactional additions were made:

i. For the purpose of joining together into a continuous whole various fragmentary pieces which had been handed down; here the redactional elements are in the nature of *connecting links*.

ii. For the purpose of emphasizing and driving home something in the text, or for enforcing the lesson of some historical event referred to in the text. These would come under the heads of *amplifications*.

iii. For the purpose of modifying or correcting something in the light of later thought. These might be termed *modifications* of something in the text.

iv. For the purpose of explaining some difficulty, or what appeared to be a difficulty in the text, i.e. *explanatory comments*.

v. For the purpose of giving vent to some emotional feeling inspired by some passage; one might call these *pious ejaculations*.

Most of the redactional elements in the books of the Old Testament will be found, we venture to think, to owe their presence in the text to one of these causes. In many cases, there can be no doubt, these additions were originally marginal notes not intended to form part of the text, but were inserted in the text by later copyists.

Finally, it may be pointed out that the grounds on which scholars are led to suspect that words or passages did not form an original part of the text are the following:

i. If they break the context or interfere with the sense of a passage.

ii. If they show a sudden difference of style, or, in the case of books written in rhythmic measure, if the rhythm is suddenly changed into a different measure, or if it ceases altogether and prose takes its place.

iii. If the style of language changes; that is particularly noticeable when words occur which belong to a later stage of Hebrew.

iv. If it is found that a passage does not occur in the Septuagint, or if the Septuagint clearly presupposes a different Hebrew text.

These, in all probability, do not cover the whole ground; but in most cases it is one or other of the above-mentioned things which leads to the belief, and often to the conviction, that certain words or a certain passage was not originally an integral part of the text.

II

THE COMPONENT PARTS OF ISAIAH XL.–LXVI., THEIR CONTENTS AND DATE

II

THE COMPONENT PARTS OF ISAIAH XL.–LXVI., THEIR CONTENTS AND DATE

We have briefly considered the reasons why Isaiah i.–xxxix. must be regarded as a composite work. This will have served as a kind of preparation and introduction to our second Lecture, in which we shall see that Isaiah xl.–lxvi. offers from a literary point of view much that we have already seen to be characteristic of the earlier division.

It will not be necessary to discuss in much detail here the reasons which have led the majority of scholars to recognize the originally separate and independent pieces of which these chapters are composed; for these reasons will, it is hoped, become apparent as we proceed. The problem is not so intricate in Isaiah xl.–lxvi. as in Isaiah i.–xxxix.; the different compositions in this second division of the book are so marked, one might almost say so obvious, in their general outlines that the ordinary intelligent reader of the English Bible can hardly fail to recognize them when once pointed out. We shall therefore simply state what the component parts consist of, and leave the contents and character of each to explain why each of these component parts must be regarded as of different authorship.

Three independent compositions make up the bulk of Isaiah xl.–lxvi., viz.:

(1) Chapters xl.–lv.
(2) The Ebed-Jahwe Songs.
(3) Chapters lvi.–lxvi.

There are, as in Isaiah i.–xxxix, a number of redactional insertions; attention will be drawn to some of these.

We have used the expression "Ebed-Jahwe" Songs for shortness and convenience' sake; *Ebed* is the Hebrew for "Servant," and *Jahwe* is the more correct form for what is transliterated *Jehovah* in the English Bible, and often translated "Lord." In the Hebrew the four letters of the divine name are JHWH. On account of the sacredness of the name, it was never pronounced,[1]

[1] It was pronounced, though in an undertone so as not to be heard by the people, when the Blessing was given,

COMPONENT PARTS OF ISAIAH XL–LXVI

but instead there were added to the four consonants the vowels belonging to the Hebrew word for "Lord," namely *Adonai* (the i here does not represent a vowel in Hebrew), and for the sacred name there was substituted Adonai; hence "Lord" in the English Bible when the word is translated, and "Jehovah" when transliterated.[1] Both are unsatisfactory; "Jehovah" is in any case an impossible form from the Hebrew point of view because it consists of the consonants of one word and the vowels of another; "Lord" is unsatisfactory as an equivalent for the Hebrew divine name because it obscures the significant fact that this is a *proper name*. The expression "Ebed-Jahwe" Songs will thus be seen to be justified. We proceed now to examine these three divisions of our book.

(1) *Chapters xl.–lv.*

As the Ebed-Jahwe Songs (see next section), interspersed among these chapters, must be regarded as of different authorship

in the name of the Lord, in the Temple by the High Priest. This information is given in the Mishna, *Joma* vi 2, *Sotah* vii. 6, *Sanhedrin* x. 1.

[1] The Hebrew letter wrongly transliterated v corresponds to our w.

from the writings in which they have become embedded, it will be understood that in dealing with chapters xl.–lv. these Songs are for the present eliminated.

A good deal of discussion has taken place among scholars on the question as to whether chapters xl.–lv. form a unity, or whether they should be regarded as constituting two separate pieces. The question is a difficult one to settle, for a good deal is to be said in favour of either contention. One important point worth bearing in mind in seeking to come to a conclusion is that while the doctrinal standpoint between the sections xl.–lv. and lvi.–lxvi. shows a marked difference, it is practically uniform throughout xl.–lv.; a fact which, at any rate, points to the whole of this section belonging to the same age. Further, the general uniformity of style and diction which marks xl.–lv. points to unity of authorship. On the other hand, one cannot fail to see that there is a difference of general outlook in the two halves into which xl.–lv. are divided, viz., in xl.–xlviii. attention is centred upon the exiles in Babylon, while in xlix.–lv. it is transferred, speaking generally, to the Jews in Palestine. Taking all things into consideration, one rather feels that the whole of xl.–lv. (exclusive of the Ebed-Jahwe Songs and some later interpolations) is by the same author, who wrote the earlier part in Babylon and the later part in Palestine, the whole section thus being dated within the years 546 B.C. and soon after 536, roughly speaking, i.e. between the time of the imminent fall of Babylon and soon after the issue of Cyrus's decree. It is objected that chapters xlix.–lv. cannot have been written in Palestine on account of the writer's lack of recognizing concrete realities—his description and general idea of the nation's condition not agreeing with its actual forlorn state—but if it be once conceded that the similarity of style and diction, as well as identity in the doctrinal standpoint, between the two parts justifies belief in unity of authorship, then one can easily understand an idealist like Deutero-Isaiah being less concerned with present realities than with an idealistic future. Indeed it is not, one would hope, an exaggeration to say that, apart from other reasons with which it is impossible to deal now, the idealism common to the two halves into which these chapters, xl.–lv., fall, almost compels one to the conclusion that they are the product of one mind. Take, for example, these two passages, one from each part, xl. 3, 4[1]:

Prepare ye in the wilderness the way of the Lord,
Make straight in the desert a highway for our God.
Every valley shall be exalted, and every mountain and hill shall be made low,
And the crooked shall be made straight, and the rough places plain;

and lii. 7–9:

How beautiful upon the mountains are the feet of him that bringeth good tidings,
That publisheth peace, that bringeth good tidings of good, that publisheth salvation;
That saith unto Zion, thy God reigneth!
The voice of thy watchman! they lift up the voice, together do they sing;
For they shall see, eye to eye, when the Lord returneth to Zion.
Break forth into joy, sing together, ye waste places of Jerusalem;
For the Lord hath comforted His people, He hath redeemed Jerusalem.

The idealism and the form into which it is

[1] Quotations are from the Revised Version unless for some special reason a closer translation of the Hebrew seems desirable.

put, which constitutes the very soul of these two passages—clearly written under different conditions, at different times, and (one cannot help feeling) in different places—strikes one as of the same mould in either passage and as emanating from the same mind. Numbers of similar examples are to be found in these two sections respectively. We may take it, therefore (though not all scholars are agreed upon the point), that the whole of xl.–lv., with the exceptions already indicated, are from the same hand, the prophet whom we called the "Second Isaiah," or Deutero-Isaiah.

(2) *The Ebed-Jahwe Songs.*

These Songs are four in number, comprised in the following passages:

xlii. 1-4, xlix. 1-6, l. 4-9, lii. 13–liii. 12.

These Songs deal exclusively with the mysterious figure known as the "Servant of the Lord," though it must be remembered that in the section of our book which we have just been considering there is also the mention of the "Servant of the Lord." Now it is an instructive study and one which cannot fail to throw light upon the relationship between these Songs and the chapters we have just been dealing with, to contrast the "Servant of the Lord" conception as presented in these two parts of our book respectively. This contrast will be seen to be the more striking if we notice first some points of similarity between the two. Thus, in each case the servant is the *chosen* of the Lord; and *therefore* the Lord's help is accorded him; in each case the servant is described as *God's witness*; his enemies, as the enemies of God, are to be annihilated. Again, the outpouring of God's spirit is mentioned in connexion with His servant in each case; but there is this difference, that in xliv. 3 His spirit is to be poured out upon His servant's *seed*, whereas in the first of the Songs it is the servant *himself* upon whom God puts His spirit (xlii. 1). Lastly, there is a glorious future promised by God to His servant in xl.-lv., and perhaps it is not fanciful to see an echo of this in the words of the last Song:

Therefore shall he inherit among the great,
And shall divide the spoil with the strong,
For he poured out his soul unto death (liii. 12).

These points of similarity between the two conceptions of the servant suggest a certain connexion originally; by saying that it is not meant to imply that the writer of the Songs is the same who wrote chapters xl.-lv., but that the conception of the servant found in these chapters formed the basis, or point of attachment, from which arose the more exalted ideas which we get in the Songs. That the two component parts are not by the same author is suggested by the contrast between the two conceptions of the servant put forth in either, as well as by the special *traits* which characterize him in the Songs. The contrasts are these: In chapters xl.-lv. the servant is the nation of Israel, while in the Songs he is an individual; in the former he is spoken of as blind and deaf, a worm, despised by the Gentiles, and sinful; in the latter he is innocent, faithful to God, and His true disciple, inspired daily by divine illumination, and obedient in following God's guidance. In both cases the servant is a sufferer; but the nation suffers through its own sins at the hands of the oppressor, while this particular and individual servant suffers for the sins of others; that is the special point of his suffering. Besides these points of contrast there are certain *traits* characteristic of the servant as depicted in the Songs which place him in an entirely different category. His humility and gentleness, his mission as the restorer of Israel, and to be a light to the Gentiles:

Too small a thing it is for thee [1] *to re-establish the tribes of Jacob
And to restore the preserved of Israel;
I will also give thee for a light to the Gentiles,
That my salvation may be unto the ends of the earth* (xlix. 6).

And, above all, his mysterious *rôle* as a sacrificial atonement. (Further reference to this last will be made in another lecture.)

In taking all these points of similarity and contrast into consideration, as well as those which give a peculiar uniqueness to the servant in the Songs, one is led to the conclusion that the servant conception of chapters xl.–lv. must be logically antecedent to that contained in the Songs, the latter being a development of the former; and that therefore the Songs are of later date than chapters xl.–lv. In this case, however, the Songs must have been inserted in the text of Deutero-Isaiah, and the question arises as

---

[1] The words "that thou shouldest be my servant" overweight the text and spoil the rhythm; they are a redactor's explanatory comment.

to why this was done. In the case of the three first Songs the reason is not difficult to discern, as will be seen by a brief examination of the contexts in which they stand.

The *First Song*, xl. 1-4 (verses 5-7 forming an appendix to it),[1] breaks into a section and is inserted after a passage beginning:

I have raised up one from the north, and he cometh,
From the rising of the sun one that calleth on my name . . . (xli. 25).

The reference here is to Cyrus, and although he is not termed the servant of the Lord, he is God's instrument and carries out His purpose, and in so far serves the Lord. But to the more spiritually-minded writer of the Songs this idea of a Gentile and an idolater being God's chosen instrument is not altogether congenial; he therefore directs the reader's thoughts to a higher conception of what God's servant must be. In contrast to the warrior's battle-shout, he describes the servant as one who "shall not cry, nor lift up, nor cause his voice to be heard in the street." In contrast to the warrior's death-

[1] These verses are in a different metre and supplement what is said in the Song; they are, therefore, not regarded as forming part of the Song by many scholars.

dealing blows, he says of the Servant: "A bruised reed shall he not break, and dimly burning flax (or 'wick') shall he not quench." In contrast to material victory it is said of this servant that, "He shall bring forth equity in truth"—also a victory, but more difficult to attain. The point of the insertion of this first Song is, therefore, clear enough; the writer's conception of the character and function of God's chosen instrument is more spiritual than that of Deutero-Isaiah; and he wishes to correct, or at all events to modify, the impression gained from the passage he had before him.

This is also true of the *Second Song* (xlix. 1-6). Like the first Song this also follows a section in which reference is made to Cyrus as God's instrument (xlviii. 1 ff.); but what is more important is that this reference is, in this case, merely accidental; the section is mainly concerned with the nation of Israel which has been called by God, but which has been unfaithful to Him. As this section now stands there are, in all probability, various later additions in it, but its form is more or less that which the writer of the Songs had before him. Although in this section the nation of Israel is not specifically called the servant of Jahwe, or "My servant," until the very end, it is quite obvious that it is regarded as such all through. This can be seen from the following words, and it is important to note the character of the nation as here described :—

Hear ye this, O house of Jacob:
Which are called by the name of Israel,
   And are come forth out of the bowels[1] *of Jacob,*
Which swear by the name of Jahwe,
   And make mention of the God of Israel—
But not in truth, nor in righteousness (xlviii. 1).

Again, in verse 4, it is said:

Because I knew that thou art obstinate,
And thy neck is an iron sinew,
And thy brow brass . . .

And once more, verse 8:

Yea, thou heardest not; thou knewest not,
Yea, from all time thine ear was not opened.

That is the character given of the nation, yet that the nation is conceived of as Jahwe's servant is obvious from the words of the same section :

---

[1] Reading מעמי instead of ממי (" waters ")

*Behold, I have refined thee, but not as silver,
I have tried thee in the furnace of affliction;
For mine own sake, mine own sake, will I do
     it . . .
  Hearken unto me, O Jacob,
  And Israel, my called one . . .* (xlviii. 10–12).

A few verses further on, some beautiful words follow, emphasizing the same thing; some scholars doubt, however, whether they originally formed part of the text, their somewhat legal character not being in the style of the writer:

*Thus saith Jahwe, thy Redeemer,
  The holy One of Israel:
I, Jahwe, am thy God,
  Which teacheth thee to profit,
Which leadeth thee in the way thou shouldest go.
  O that thou hadst hearkened unto my commandments!
Then had thy peace been as a river,
  And thy righteousness as the waves of the
     sea . . .* (xlviii. 17–19).

Then at the end of the section come the words:

*Say ye, Jahwe hath redeemed
His servant Jacob.*

Now it is abundantly clear that the servant here described falls short in many respects, and that such a conception was not likely to be a source of inspiration to the people. Therefore the Second Song is added here. And in this Song, the servant, so far from being a cause of dishonour to God, as the nation, Jahwe's servant, had been

(Which swear by Jahwe's name,
 And make mention of the God of Israel,
But not in truth,
Nor in righteousness),

is spoken of as one to whom God says:

Thou art my Servant,[1]
In whom I will be glorified (xlix. 3).

Whereas in the preceding verses Israel is spoken of as not obeying God's commandment, in this Song, although the Servant says in humility:

I have laboured in vain,
I have spent my strength for nought and vanity,

he adds:

Yet, surely my judgement is with Jahwe,
 And my recompense with my God (verse 4).

[1] The word "Israel" is obviously an addition, see verse 5

And a little later on his great mission is proclaimed:

*Too small a thing it is for thee to re-establish the tribes of Jacob,
And to restore the preserved of Israel;
I will also give thee for a light to the Gentiles,
That my salvation may be unto the ends of the earth* (verse 6).

The purpose of the insertion of this Song in the place where it now stands can again be fully explained by regarding it as a second example of the desire to present a more exalted conception of the servant of the Lord than that of Deutero-Isaiah.

Coming now to the *Third Song* (l. 4–9), it will be noticed that its presence in the place in which it stands cannot be accounted for in the way in which the two preceding songs can; there is no mention in the context of a servant; it is true, in verse 10, which immediately follows the Song, occur the words:

*Who among you feareth Jahwe,
Let him obey the voice of His Servant?*

But, for reasons which cannot be gone into here, there is a general consensus among scholars that verses 10, 11 form a later appendix to the Song itself. The reason why the Song was inserted here is probably because in the verses immediately preceding it the nation is rebuked for its want of faith; nobody has come forward to co-operate in the work with Jahwe because they did not believe in His power :

Wherefore, when I came, was there no man,
When I called was there none to answer? (l. 2).

Here then, it seemed, was an appropriate place to insert an Ebed-Jahwe Song, in order to show that though Israel was unbelieving and weak, that there was yet one who was a true servant; he is described thereupon in this Song that follows; and it must be looked upon as constituting a corrective, as well as an encouragement to the nation. It is noticeable that in contrast to the want of faith and the weakness described in the verses immediately preceding the Song we have in the Song itself just the converse of these two things described as characteristics of the Servant of Jahwe :

I was not rebellious,
Nor turned away backward . . . (verse 5)
For the Lord Jahwe doth help me,
Therefore am I not confounded;

Therefore do I set my face like a flint;
And I knew that I should not be ashamed.
He is near that justifieth me, who will contend
  with me?
  Let us stand up together!
Who is mine adversary?
  Let him come near to me!
Behold, Jahwe helpeth me,
  Who will condemn me? . . . (verses 7–11).

As regards the *Fourth*, the great, Song (lii. 13–liii. 12), it is true that there does not appear to be any point of attachment either in what precedes or follows, i.e. in its *immediate* context; nevertheless, its presence in this book—whatever reason the compiler may have had in inserting it in the particular place it now occupies—is of great significance. But this point is dealt with below,[1] where the doctrinal teaching of the Song is considered. We shall therefore postpone for the present any further study of the Song.

These Ebed-Jahwe Songs, then, must be regarded as separate compositions, the style, thought and teaching of which stamp them as having all been written by the same author. A later compiler inserted them into the text of Deutero-Isaiah with the object of infusing

[1] See pp. 88 ff.

COMPONENT PARTS OF ISAIAH XL–LXVI

into the book a deeper spirituality. That the four Songs are all that are left of what was once a much larger collection belonging to the same author cannot be proved; but that this represents the facts of the case seems probable if for no other reason than this, that one does not understand how such a writer on such a subject could have restricted himself to the four short Songs which have come down to us.

(3) *Chapters lvi.–lxvi.*

That the historical background of these chapters is different from the rest of the book is pretty obvious. We shall not go into any of the details of this here,[1] but merely point out that Persian rule is now a settled thing; the golden hopes of Deutero-Isaiah are unfulfilled, and the reason for this is ascribed to the presence of godless and heretical people within the Jewish community. There is no longer any question of a return from captivity, for the Jews are settled in their own land. Their condition, both religious and social, is very unsatisfactory. Hypocritical worship (lviii. 1 ff.), formalism, oppression of the godly, and wickedness of all kinds is prevalent among

[1] See Lecture VI.

the people. The passage lix. 1 ff., e.g., is full of terrible condemnation :

Behold, Jahwe's hand is not shortened, that it
  cannot save ;
His ear is not heavy, that it cannot hear ;
But your iniquities have separated between you
  and your God,
And your sins caused His face to be hidden from
  you (that He will not hear).
For your hands are defiled with blood,
And your fingers with iniquity ;
Your lips have spoken lies,
Your tongue muttereth wickedness.
None sueth in righteousness,
And none pleadeth in truth ;
They conceive mischief,
They bring forth iniquity !

Such are the conditions which are referred to again and again in these chapters. Then, further, although the Temple has been rebuilt, there is the threat on the part of some to build a rival temple, thus revealing the presence of schismatics. The reason of the existence of this is opposition to the *Law* on the part of many. This fact gives both a clear indication of the approximate date of these chapters, and also shows us that they belong to the period in which Judaism was becoming transformed. This, as we shall see in another lecture, gives great importance to these chapters from a doctrinal point of view. It was in 458 B.C. that Ezra returned to Jerusalem with a band of exiles; and his fixed intention was to make the observance of the Law, as he understood it, paramount among his people. There are some indications in these chapters that he had grave difficulties to contend with, e.g.:

I have spread out my hands all the day
  Unto a rebellious people;
Which walketh in a way that is not good
  After their own thoughts (lxv. 2).

That way is not the way of the Law. The *right* "way" is the way of the Law, as we know well enough from other books, e.g., *Blessed are they that are perfect in the way, who walk in the Law of the Lord* (Ps. cxix. 1.); *Teach me, O Lord, the way of thy statutes and I shall keep it unto the end* (verse 33), etc. etc. But though Ezra and his followers met with difficulties and opposition at first, he succeeded later on with the help of Nehemiah, who returned in 445 B.C. And in these chapters, as we shall see in another lecture, there are many indications of the rise of the newer Judaism; the Judaism of the New Testament, and the Judaism which consequently exercised a great influence on Christian doctrine. To this we shall, of course, devote special attention.

From what has been said, we may take it that these chapters belong more or less to the middle of the fifth century B.C., but after 450 rather than before.

With the exception of small redactional additions these chapters form a unity; but while they come from the same book, it is improbable that they were all written at the same time; there are signs in the book that the author's doctrinal standpoint underwent modification. We look in vain for much originality of thought in these chapters; the author draws largely from Deutero-Isaiah and Ezekiel, sometimes he quotes verbally from the former; and, moreover, introduces three pieces constructed on a pattern similar to that of the Ebed-Jahwe Songs inserted in Deutero-Isaiah (viz. lxi. 1-4; lxii. 1; lxii. 6, 7). It will be unnecessary to say more about these chapters here as they will receive special attention in lecture vi.

III

A BRIEF SURVEY OF THE HISTORICAL BACKGROUND OF ISAIAH XL.–XLVI.

III

A BRIEF SURVEY OF THE HISTORICAL BACKGROUND OF ISAIAH XL.–LXVI.

FROM what has been said it will have been seen that the dates of the different compositions of which these chapters are made up cover a considerable period of time ; and if, as must be done, we take into consideration the work of the redactor, the period is still further extended, though with this last, the Grecian, period it will not be necessary to deal in this survey. Definiteness in assigning dates to biblical documents is not possible excepting in rare cases, though it is generally, but not always, possible to give an *approximate* date with reasonable certitude. It will therefore be well in this brief historical survey to take a glance at the *whole period* within the limits of which the different compositions of Isaiah xl.–lxvi. fall, though in doing so some epochs will doubtlessly be embraced within our purview, with which these compositions have nothing to do.

(1) *Judæa after the Fall of Jerusalem and during the Captivity.*

It will be well to cast a brief glance, by way of introduction, back to the time immediately preceding the Babylonian exile. The actual number of those carried away captive by Nebuchadrezzar was not great. We have in Jeremiah lii. 28–30 an enumeration of the captives, together with the dates of their being carried away, which inspires confidence by its moderation and exactness: *This is the people whom Nebuchadrezzar carried away captive: in the seventh year* (i.e. 598 B.C.) *three thousand Jews and three and twenty; in the eighteenth year of Nebuchadrezzar* (i.e. 587 B.C.) *he carried away captive from Jerusalem eight hundred thirty and two persons; in the three and twentieth year of Nebuchadrezzar* (i.e. 582 B.C.) *Nebuzar-adan the captain of the guard carried away captive of the Jews seven hundred forty and five persons; all the persons were four thousand and six hundred.*[1] This number refers, in all probability, to men only, for in giving numbers the Old Testament only reckons men;[2] so that the actual number

---

[1] This is a more reliable number than that given in 2 Kings xxiv 14, 16

[2] As is still the custom in the East

THE HISTORICAL BACKGROUND 51

of souls would have been not less than four times as many. On the other hand, it is evident from Ezekiel xxiv. 21 that entire families did not in every case go away together, for the prophet speaks of "your sons and your daughters whom ye have left behind." But though the number of exiles was comparatively small, the quality of those who were taken from their country was most significant; the passage referring to this (2 Kings xxiv. 14-16) may be to some extent an exaggeration, but the essence of it is undoubtedly historical: *And he carried away all Jerusalem, and all the princes, and all the mighty men of valour, even ten thousand captives, and all the craftsmen and the smiths ; none remained save the poorest sort of the people of the land* . . . (cp. xxv. 12). In addition to those transported to Babylon, it must be remembered that a certain number, and among them evidently some of the influential people of the land, migrated voluntarily to Egypt (2 Kings xxv. 26).

After the fall of Jerusalem the condition of the Jews who were left in Judæa was a sad one ; bereft of most of their natural leaders and even of those who might have taken their places, the people, composed for the most part of the poorer classes, found themselves in a state of helplessness. But this would assuredly have been remedied in course of time ; sooner or later new leaders would have been forthcoming from among the people and have raised the country at any rate to a moderate state of prosperity once more, even though under the suzerainty of the king of Babylon. This was however, not to be. And it was largely owing to Nebuchadrezzar's choice of the successor to Jehoiachin who had been dethroned and taken to Babylon. In his place Nebuchadrezzar placed Mattaniah [1] on the throne of Judah. The position of a king of Judah was at this time one of peculiar difficulty ; it needed a man of special gifts, of vigour on the one hand, of tact on the other ; for he had to raise his people from the slough of despair, and yet to remember that he was a vassal of the mighty king of Babylon. While, under the circumstances, it would have been impossible for the land to have played any independent part among the nations, it might yet, under the ægis of Babylon, have filled a not inconsiderable *rôle* in the international politics of the times. But for this loyalty to the suzerain power would have

---

[1] He changed his name to Zedekiah on coming to the throne (2 Kings xxiv. 17).

THE HISTORICAL BACKGROUND 53

been a prime necessity for such a weak state as Judah now was. To nourish the innate vigour of the people and to encourage obedience among them to the over-lord would have been as beneficial to the country as farsighted from the political standpoint. If such a *rôle* were for the present humble it would none the less have been a preparation for better times ; and Babylon was no more invincible than Assyria had been. Zedekiah, however, lacked strength of character, and was wanting in statesmanship. He thought to have been able to throw off the yoke of Babylon ; he failed and suffered the penalty. *Then they took the king, and carried him up unto the king of Babylon to Riblah; and they gave judgement upon him. And they slew the sons of Zedekiah before his eyes, and put out the eyes of Zedekiah, and bound him in fetters, and carried him to Babylon* (2 Kings xxv. 6, 7) ; he remained in prison till the day of his death (Jer. lii. 11). In his place a governor, Gedaliah, was placed in control of the country ; he made Mizpah his headquarters and tried to organize and rule the land as a Babylonian province. It was, however, not long before he was put to death by the Jews. We are not told who Gedaliah's successor was, but the pitiable condition to which the land was now reduced is tragically described in the second and fourth chapters of the book of Lamentations.

(2) *The Exiles in Babylon.*

When in 597 B.C. a number of Jews were deported to Babylon it was evidently not thought that their absence would be of long duration; a speedy return was prophesied by various prophets. Among them Hananiah encouraged false hopes among the people by uttering this prophecy: *Thus speaketh the Lord of hosts, the God of Israel, saying, I have broken the yoke of the king of Babylon. Within two full years will I bring again into this place all the vessels of the Lord's house, that Nebuchadnezzar king of Babylon took away from this place, and carried them to Babylon; and I will bring again to this place Jeconiah the son of Jehoiakim king of Judah, with all the captives of Judah, that went to Babylon, saith the Lord; for I will break the yoke of the king of Babylon* (Jer. xxviii. 1-4, cp. verse 15; see also xxvii. 14 ff.). If, as is more than probable, the report of such prophecies came to the ears of the exiles,[1] with

---

[1] Intercourse between the exiles and the people of Judæa was at first frequent (see Jer. xxix 1 ff 25, li 59, Ezek.

THE HISTORICAL BACKGROUND 55

the result that they looked for a speedy return, their disappointment and consternation must have been great when they heard of the fall of Jerusalem in 587. It was then time for them to recall and act upon the counsel which Jeremiah had given some years previously: *Thus saith the Lord of hosts, the God of Israel, unto all the captivity, whom I have caused to be carried away captive from Jerusalem unto Babylon: Build ye houses, and dwell in them; and plant gardens, and eat the fruit of them; take ye wives and beget sons and daughters; and take wives for your sons, and give your daughters to husbands, that they may bear sons and daughters; and multiply ye there, and be not diminished. And seek the peace of the city whither I have caused you to be carried away captive, and pray unto the Lord for it; for in the peace thereof shall ye have peace* (Jer. xxix. 4–7). It is evident from these words that the prophet did not anticipate for his people a very hard lot in the land of their captivity; and the *data* which have come down to us regarding the condition of the Jews there show that the expectation was not disappointed. The references which the prophet Ezekiel

xxiv. 26); after the fall of Jerusalem it ceased almost entirely.

makes to the general conditions of life do not suggest hardship; quite the contrary, see Ezekiel i. 3; viii. 1; see also Ezra viii. 15–21. The people had great freedom within the limits of the kingdom, and they were permitted full exercise of their religion. In this latter a profound alteration began to take place; instead of the sacrificial system which had hitherto been the main religious expression of Israel, but which could now no more be practised, the leaders were led to think of the deeper truths of religion: the problem of sin, personal responsibility, the meaning of suffering, atonement, a fuller apprehension of God and of His majesty. Not that some external requirements were forgotten; circumcision and the observance of the Sabbath became the distinguishing marks of the Jews. The rise of the *Sopherim* (Scribes), which took place during the Exile, denoted another sphere of activity, viz. the copying and editing of the biblical books; these were edited in the light of the Law as represented, above all, by the book of Deuteronomy.

The Exile had lasted nearly fifty years when Cyrus II, king of Persia, conquered Astyages, king of the Medes, and became ruler of the entire Median kingdom. This

THE HISTORICAL BACKGROUND 57

was about 550 B.C. In the year 547 he overthrew Croesus, king of Lydia, and incorporated this land into his empire. It was these brilliant victories which caused the prophet whom we call Deutero-Isaiah to see in Cyrus God's instrument for the delivering of the Jews from their Babylonian masters, and of restoring them to their native land. Cyrus's victories were crowned by the capture of Babylon, though (it is true) he met with no serious resistance here. He made Babylon his place of residence, and treated the people kindly. He also accepted the religion of the newly-conquered country and worshipped the gods of Babylon. The ancient religion of Persia permitted Cyrus not only to respect the religions of other peoples but also to foster them. Thanks to this he showed sympathy for the religion of the Jews, and gave command that the Temple in Jerusalem should be rebuilt on hearing that this had fallen into ruin. He also appointed Sheshbazzar, a Jew, governor of Judæa and sent him to Jerusalem to see to the carrying-out of his commands. Sheshbazzar laid the foundation-stone of the Temple in Jerusalem and began the building (see Ezra v. 13-16). Although our records do not definitely say so, it is probable that a person of Sheshbazzar's importance would have been accompanied by other subordinate officials and a sufficient retinue ; moreover, as we shall see presently, the political state of Palestine was such that the envoy of the Persian king would require to be invested with all the outward marks of authority in order to impress the turbulent peoples into whose midst he was about to come.

(3) *The Jews in Palestine after the Return.*

The arrival of Sheshbazzar in Jerusalem was the first event in post-exilic times which began to stir up the Jews of Palestine from the torpor in which they had lain for a couple of generations. From direct statements in our sources and from what seems to be implied we can picture the political state of the country at this time to have been approximately as follows : in the north the Samaritans—i.e. a mixed race composed of the remnants of the inhabitants of the northern kingdom left behind by the Assyrian conquerors (722 B.C.), and Assyrian colonists who had been settled down there by the king of Assyria [1]—were in possession. In

---

[1] *And the king of Assyria brought men from Babylon, and from Cuthah and from Ava, and from Hamath and Sepharvaim, and placed them in the cities of Samaria instead of the children*

THE HISTORICAL BACKGROUND 59

the south the Edomites, through the pressure of the Arabians on the south-east of Jordan pushing northwards, had entered into and taken possession of the country up to and including Hebron.[1] A tract of country lying to the north of the Dead Sea had been taken by the Ammonites, who had also come from the east of Jordan. Finally, on the western border were the Philistines who had never shown themselves friendly neighbours to the Jews. There was no question of driving out all these alien elements since the power to do so was wholly lacking to Sheshbazzar; so that one can fully realize the difficulty which lay before the new governor of Judæa in seeking to resuscitate his nation, surrounded as he was by unfriendly and jealous peoples. He and his followers were thus compelled to restrict their activity to Jerusalem and the immediately surrounding districts. This, however, was all that was required; for, as far as the returned exiles were concerned, their entire thoughts and activities were centred on religion. Their firm belief was that when once Jahwe's

of Israel; and they possessed Samaria, and dwelt in the cities thereof (2 Kings xvii 24, cp. Ezra iv. 2, 10).
[1] I.e., the country known later as Idumæa.

altar was again set up and His ancient worship was revived, the Messianic Era would break in and all would be well. Disappointment, however, awaited them; things did not turn out as had been expected; without and within arose anxiety and worry. It was a time of sad disillusionment, as can be fully seen from the biblical writings which refer to these times, see especially Hag. i. 6, 10, 11; Zech. viii. 10. It is little wonder that in the stress of the times the zeal for rebuilding the Temple which had at first animated the returned exiles grew cold; disappointed hopes had chilled their hearts. Moreover, owing to the intrigues of their enemies it appears that they were forced to suspend the building.

Years rolled on during which the people were sunk in dull resignation. Then, suddenly, a reawakening came. The advent of the Messiah, which had been so long vainly looked for, was seen to be actually taking place; for Zerubbabel, the successor of Sheshbazzar, was proclaimed to be the expected Messiah. This was the declaration of the prophets whose voices were raised again. They appeared in Jerusalem and bade the people set to work again on the

THE HISTORICAL BACKGROUND 61

Temple, for the Messianic Era was now about to dawn, God was about to punish the nations, and Israel was coming to his own. This occurred in 520 B.C., and what gave rise to the new ferment was the state of affairs in the Persian kingdom. Late in the year 521 Darius overthrew and slew the usurper Gaumata, and became king. But this sudden and vigorous action created great unrest throughout the kingdom, each race looking for some advantage in the troubled times ; Medes, Babylonians, Armenians, Parthians, and various other smaller races, rose up against the new king. It was a most critical time for Darius, and it looked as though the world were going to be turned upside down. The Judæan leaders gazed with eagerness at what was taking place. But by the spring of the year 519 Darius had already overcome all his enemies and was securely seated on his throne. The Messianic expectations of the Jews were again disappointed. One advantage they gained ; they were permitted to recommence the building of the Temple ; this was done with renewed vigour, and the second Temple, or the Temple of Zerubbabel, was completed in the spring of the year 516 B.C. But even this long looked-for event did not bring with it the expected results; our sources present us with a sad picture of the want of religious fervour, of externalism in worship, of tyranny among the wealthier classes, and want and discontent among the poor. Mixed marriages resulted in introducing heathen customs; the religion of Jahwe became polluted, as so often before in the history of the people. This state of affairs went on for many years. To combat all this a party was gradually formed of the better elements among the people, who sought by warnings and the utterance of impending judgement in the " day of the Lord " to bring the renegades to a better state of mind. This conflict was followed with intense interest by the Jews who were still resident in Babylon, above all by the religious leader there, Ezra. We may well believe a great preparation went on there to bring about a drastic reformation in Jerusalem when the time should come and opportunity should offer. Nor was this time far distant. The king was approached and his permission was obtained for this reform party in Babylon to return under Ezra to Jerusalem. The party, consisting of 1,760 men and their families, together with priests

THE HISTORICAL BACKGROUND 63

and Levites, arrived in the year 458 B.C. Ezra set to work with great vigour with his reforms, but though at first he met with some measure of success, his attempts ultimately failed, and it was not until the arrival of Nehemiah with a further number of the exiles in 445 B.C. that the reform party got the upper hand. The nature of this reform is clearly indicated in Neh. viii.-x.; its essence is contained in the words of Neh. x. 28, 29: *And the rest of the people, the priests, the Levites . . . they clave to their brethren, their nobles, and entered into a curse, and into an oath, to walk in God's law, which was given by Moses the servant of God, and to observe and do all the commandments of the Lord our Lord, and his judgements and his statutes.* Thus was introduced a new epoch in the history of the Jews, above all in the religious history of the Jews; it was the beginning of the new Judaism.

IV

THE DOCTRINAL STANDPOINT OF ISAIAH XL.–LV.

IV

THE DOCTRINAL STANDPOINT OF ISAIAH XL.–LV

WE have seen that Isaiah xl.–lxvi. is made up of three component parts, each from the hand of a different author, each of different date. In considering, therefore, the doctrinal standpoint of these chapters each component part must be treated separately. Indeed, we shall see that the difference of doctrinal standpoint in each part affords, of itself, a strong argument in favour of different authorship.

It is necessary at the outset to insist on the fact that in all these chapters, though more especially in lvi.–lxvi., the outstanding doctrines, with which alone we can concern ourselves here, are in a state of transition. Old views are beginning to be modified and new views are beginning to force themselves to the fore. The altogether new conditions under which the flower of the more spiritual and intellectual classes of the Jews lived brought new religious experiences and new religious problems which demanded long thought and speculation to apprehend, if, indeed, they were ever apprehended. We shall therefore not be surprised, rather we shall expect to find some measure of indefiniteness in some cases, a tentative and uncertain presentment, at times, rather than clear-cut and definitely-formulated dogma. There is, however, in this a very great human interest; for one seems to see sometimes in these chapters, when reading between the lines, that the writer was faced with some of the religious difficulties which many people at the present day have to face, and, like him, face unsuccessfully; that is to say, the solution of the difficulty is not apparent, and a *pis aller* has got to be put up with. However this may be, the indefiniteness and tentativeness in doctrinal standpoint sometimes to be discerned in these chapters must be our justification for allowing ourselves a larger latitude in the way of inference than would be permissible in books of the Bible in which clear-cut beliefs are taken for granted or definitely formulated; also we may be allowed some freedom in forming conclusions based on implication. It is fully realized there are dangers and pitfalls in this; but where the ground is uncertain we must be prepared to take risks. Fortunately no mistake is fatal, at least not when we are prepared to modify a conclusion in the light of fuller knowledge and instructed criticism.

(1) *The Doctrine of Atonement.*

At the very opening of these chapters the prophet, speaking in the name of God, bids the people be comforted because their captivity is drawing to an end (xl. 1, 2), their time of servitude (or "service") is accomplished, that their "iniquity is pardoned" (we shall come back to that phrase immediately), and that they have received of the Lord's hand double for all their sins. That is to say, the punishment which the people have undergone is now sufficient to atone for the sins on account of which the punishment was inflicted. The phrase "her iniquity is pardoned" is misleading. It does not represent the original (נִרְצָה עֲוֹנָהּ). The Hebrew root רצה (translated "pardoned") is used of *accepting sacrifices*, in reference to God, e.g., Hosea viii. 13: "As for the sacrifices of mine offerings, they sacrifice flesh and eat it; but the Lord accepteth them not; now will he remember their iniquity, and visit their sins" (cp. 2 Sam. xxiv. 23; Deut. xxxiii. 11, etc.). It means that a sacrifice has been accepted in payment of a debt, as it were, incurred by sin against God; and this payment of a sacrifice makes atonement. In this passage before us, therefore, it is not "iniquity pardoned" as in the ordinary way we should understand this, but "iniquity paid for," and *therefore* remitted. But the "payment" (and this is the point) in this case is not a sacrifice in the ordinary Old Testament sense, but the time of slavery, or enforced labour (wrongly rendered "warfare" in the Revised Version), suffered by the people during the Captivity; that it is which constitutes the "payment." *What they have suffered is accepted as an atonement for their sin, and the sin is therefore remitted.* So that we have here an adumbration, at the very least, of the doctrine that suffering atones for the sin of the sufferer. This is a doctrine frequently taught in later Judaism, being based upon and developed from passages similar to that which we are considering. This is worth some little illustration. In later

DOCTRINAL STANDPOINT OF XL–LV 71

Judaism it is taught, in conformity with this passage, that suffering is not only a punishment for sin, but itself the means of obliterating sin. The committing of a sin is like the incurring of a debt; when payment is made the debt is liquidated, and the matter is settled. But among the various forms that the payment can take is that of suffering, i.e., the debt to God incurred by sinning against Him can be paid by means of suffering; for example, it is said that a man should rejoice more in chastisements than in prosperity, because if he enjoyed prosperity all the days of his life the sins of which he was guilty would not be forgiven him. How, it is asked, can he attain forgiveness? He is forgiven by means of chastisements (*Sifre* 73 *b*). The matter is put very baldly in another midrash (*Pesikta* 161 *b*), where it is said that God causes the righteous to pay Him what they owe Him on account of their evil deeds, by means of suffering. And, once more, in the midrash *Bereshith Rabba* 65, we are told that Isaac prayed that he might be granted sufferings in order to turn away from him the judgement in the world to come; and in the same midrash, 5, it is said: "Suffering is more apt than sacrifice to win God's favour, and to atone for man."

But to return to Deutero-Isaiah. The passage just considered deals with one side of the doctrine of Atonement which, taken by itself, is distinctly dangerous since it implies that the obliteration of sin can be brought about by man's act.

There is, however, another side to this doctrine, and it is illustrated by xliii. 22–xliv. 5, the essence of the whole, however, being contained in xliii. 25. The passage begins by a reminder to the Jewish people that they had offered no sacrifices to God, namely, during the Captivity; the words are not to be understood in the sense of a rebuke because, of course, the people could not be expected to observe the sacrificial system during the exile. The words are meant firstly, as a statement of fact; but secondly, and what is more important, they imply the non-necessity of sacrifices as a means of atoning for sin, because in verse 25 come the words: *I, even I, am he that blotteth out thy transgressions, and I will not remember thy sins.*[1] The stress laid upon the

---

[1] The addition of the words " for my own sake " in the Hebrew was probably not in the original text, for they

DOCTRINAL STANDPOINT OF XL–LV

personal pronoun—" I, even I,"—is significant ; and the rest of the passage emphasizes the way in which God's grace and mercy are accorded to the nation, though they are wholly unmerited. A striking symbolic picture is presented : just as the parched land is refreshed with rain and brings forth abundant fruit in consequence—the land itself being, of course, unable to produce anything until first refreshed from above—so is the spirit of God shed upon His people and thereby they are enabled to be faithful to Him :

For I will pour water upon the thirsty (land),
And streams upon the dry ground ;
I will pour my spirit upon thy seed,
And my blessing upon thine offspring ;
And they shall spring up as grass amidst waters (amended text),
As willows by the watercourses (xliv. 3, 4).

The whole passage teaches, therefore, that not sacrifices, but divine love, freely given by God, obliterates sin, and thereby enables men to love and serve Him.

These two passages—there are, of course, others—are the most significant and important in the whole of Deutero-Isaiah so far as the

mar the rhythm of the passage, and are omitted by some of the most important Septuagint manuscripts.

doctrine of Atonement and Forgiveness are concerned. They may seem, from one point of view, to be mutually contradictory; but in truth they are complementary to each other. It is interesting to find that already here the doctrine of the need of works and the doctrine of justification by faith are found to be not incompatible.

(2) *The Doctrine of God.*

The particular point of interest and importance in the doctrine of God as presented in Isaiah xl.-lv. is that two conceptions of the divine characteristics appear which, as in the case of the doctrine of Atonement, are at first sight, at all events, quite incompatible with each other. On the one hand divine transcendentalism is taught, on the other a conception of God quite the reverse of this; a deeply spiritual belief together with some anthropomorphic conceptions which seem to be altogether derogatory to the majesty of God. It is true, this strange combination does not appear here in the Old Testament for the first time; most of the books betray it in some measure; none more than the Psalms.[1] But the special interest of finding

[1] Cp. the writer's *Life, Death, and Immortality; Studies*

it in this book is that it is post-exilic, and we are on the threshold of the Judaism as it was in Christian times. Isaiah xl.–lv. reflects the first beginnings of what became in some respects almost a new religion; above all, the conception of God and of the divine characteristics, based in the first instance upon the teaching of the prophets, began to assume a more speculative character. We only get adumbrations of this, it is true; but read in the light of later developments there seem to be in this book signs that the thoughts of God were beginning to take a somewhat different form from what had been the case hitherto. While the anthropomorphisms are there, the transcendental character of the Almighty finds more concentrated expression.

In later Judaism these opposing conceptions are constantly in evidence; indeed, they tend to become more exaggerated. On the one hand, God is represented as receding more and more from the world and the affairs of men; withdrawing into the inner heavens as though to shut out human access to Him. On the other hand, an

in the Psalms, pp. 1 ff., where this dual element in the doctrine of God is worked out.

intimacy is represented as having been established between God and His creatures which to modern ears sounds grossly irreverent. We may wonder at this; nevertheless, is it not a fact that something of the same kind is not infrequently in evidence in some types of popular Christianity?—The question is worth pondering as to whether, and in how far, in men's conception of God, the inevitable tendency to fuse the divine and the human is due to man's inability to conceive of God otherwise, or to a fundamental and essential truth to which man involuntarily, though inadequately, bears witness?—In any case, if only in view of this question, Deutero-Isaiah's presentation of the doctrine of God is worth a little attention.

It is undoubtedly one of the main doctrinal standpoints of Deutero-Isaiah that his conception of God is, on the one hand, strikingly exalted. Again and again he speaks of God's uniqueness, His transcendence and His holiness, and righteousness, as the Eternal One, as Creator of Heaven and earth:

I am God, and there is none else,
I am God, and none is like me (xlvi. 9, cp. xlv. 21 ff.).

I am the first, I also am the last (xlviii. 12,

DOCTRINAL STANDPOINT OF XL–LV

cp. xli. 4, xliv. 6); the phrase " the Holy One of Israel " occurs frequently; *I am the Lord that maketh all things* (xliv. 24).

For thus saith Jahwe,
  That created the Heavens ;
He is God
  That formed the earth and made it . . .
I, Jahwe, speak in righteousness,
I declare the things that are right (xlv. 18, 19).

Similar passages could be multiplied to a large extent ; but that is unnecessary. There is, however, another indication of the prophet's belief in the divine transcendence, and this is of importance in view of the teaching of later Judaism ; it is also a sign of external influence in the domain of religious belief. In the beginning of the book occur the well-known words :

The voice of one that crieth : Prepare ye
  in the wilderness
  The way of Jahwe.
Make straight in the desert
  A highway for our God.
Every valley shall be exalted,
  And every mountain and hill made low [1]
                              (xl. 3, 4).

[1] The last two lines ought probably to be transposed according to the metre.

Now even though we suppose that these words are to be taken in a figurative and not in a literal sense (though this may be questioned), there must nevertheless have been at the back of the prophet's mind some definite conception with regard to what he was saying ; there must have been a mental picture in correspondence with which he formulated his words and his message. This is obvious as soon as one comes to analyse the words. *The voice of one that crieth ;* whose voice ? Not the voice of God, because the voice says : . . . *make straight in the desert a highway for* OUR GOD ; yet not the voice of one of the people, otherwise one would have to suppose that the task to be done was to be undertaken by men, and this is obviously an impossibility,—*every valley shall be exalted, and every mountain and hill shall be made low !*—that would have been inconceivable by human hands, at all events in those days. No, the voice is that of an angelic being, who calls to his fellows to undertake the making of a pathway for Jahwe. The prophet *expects* a miraculous undertaking ; his exalted conception of God impels him to expect this, and at the same time forbids him to suppose that God should *personally*

DOCTRINAL STANDPOINT OF XL–LV

do it. Therefore he takes for granted that this miraculous occurrence will be accomplished by angelic beings; superhuman on the one hand, but, on the other, not divine. Belief in the activity of angels was, of course, prevalent in earlier days among the Israelites, but taken together with the conception of the divine transcendence and holiness so characteristic of this book it is permissible to see in this prophet's belief in angelic activity—especially the *kind* of activity here conceived of—the influence of external, i.e. Babylonian, belief. We shall have to return to this subject again later on.

But in spite of this exalted conception of God in the book there are various passages in it which show that the prophet cannot divest himself of certain other ideas concerning the Deity which are of a different order. In the first place,—though one quite realizes that a difference of opinion may exist here—one cannot help feeling that the contrast which Deutero-Isaiah so pointedly draws between God and the idols of the Gentiles betrays what is really an inadequate conception of God; e.g.:

I am Jahwe,
That is my name;

My glory, I give to no other,
Nor my praise unto graven images (xlii. 8).

Or again:

> *Senseless are they that carry*
>   *The wood of their graven image,*
> *And pray unto a God*
>   *That cannot save* (xlv. 20).

And especially such a passage as this:

Produce your cause,
  Saith Jahwe;
Bring forth your strong reasons,
  Saith Jacob's King.
Let them come forth and declare to us
  What shall happen.
Declare ye the former things, what they be,
  That we may consider them,
  And know the issue of them;
Or shew us things for to come.
Declare the things that shall come hereafter,
That we may know that ye are gods;
Yea, do good or do evil,
That together we may be amazed in seeing it (xli. 21-24).

Such and other similar passages which suggest a comparison between God and heathen idols are possibly faint echoes of times when it was really believed that nations had their national gods. But, however that may be, one would rather imagine that where otherwise such a high conception of God is found, as in this book, there would be no mention of God at all in passages in which idols were spoken of. Belief in God's transcendent character, such as Deutero-Isaiah had, would forbid, one would have thought, the utterance of the name of God in such surroundings. That one does find this to be the case (quite apart from other passages of a more directly anthropomorphic character) e.g., xlii. 14, suggests that together with his exalted belief there were yet lingering in the mind of Deutero-Isaiah conceptions about God of a less spiritual, an anthropomorphic, kind. This is altogether to be expected; the reason why attention is drawn to it is that it helps us to understand the doctrine of God in later Judaism, where we find the most exalted and spiritual conceptions intermingled with very *naïve* and childlike ideas about God and His supposed doings in heaven and on earth. We find the same thing in popular Christianity. The remarks so often heard as to why God does this, that, and the other, how He can permit one thing or another; why He allows such and such another one to suffer,—show that unthinking Christians, and apparently they include the vast bulk, have the most weird notions regarding the Deity. Deutero-Isaiah's conception of God is, of course, immeasurably above that of the ordinary Christian; but one cannot help seeing that he, too, sometimes implies ideas which are difficult to reconcile with a purely spiritual belief.

So we may conclude with the remark with which we started this subject, that the question is worth pondering as to whether, and in how far, in men's conception of God, the inevitable tendency to fuse the divine and the human is due to man's inability to conceive of God otherwise, or to a fundamental and essential truth to which man involuntarily, though inadequately, bears witness! In other words, are anthropomorphisms due to the fact that man, being human, cannot help, to some extent, imputing to God the human way of acting,—or are they an instinctive, unconscious, and very halting witness to the later revealed truth of the divine and human nature of Jesus Christ?

V

THE DOCTRINAL STANDPOINT OF THE EBED-JAHWE SONGS

V

THE DOCTRINAL STANDPOINT OF THE EBED-JAHWE SONGS

WITH the first three of these Songs (xlii. 1-4, xlix. 1-6, l. 4-9) we shall have little or nothing to say here; our attention will be fixed on the last (lii. 13-liii. 12), and we shall restrict ourselves in the main to the doctrine of Atonement and those subjects which belong inseparably to it, and in so far as this very important passage refers to them. Before coming to these, however, it is necessary to touch in the briefest way upon a point which is not without its bearing on the main subject to be studied. While it is fully realized that many scholars hold the contrary view, we maintain that one cannot lay too much stress on the *individuality* of the " Servant of the Lord "[1] as he is presented in all these Songs, but, above all, in the one upon which we shall

[1] We use this form of the title as being the more familiar.

concentrate attention. It seems to us that one has but to read such verses as lii. 14, liii. 8, 9, 10, not to mention others, to realize the inappropriateness, not to use a stronger word, of regarding the "Servant of the Lord" as other than an individual. It is interesting to note that the normal Jewish view regards the Servant in all these passages as standing for the nation of Israel; nevertheless, in the Targum to the Prophets, wherever in this Song there is a reference to the humiliation of the Servant it is interpreted of the nation of Israel, but wherever the glory of the Servant is spoken of (as e.g. in liii. 10-12) it is interpreted of the Messiah. On the other hand, in an interesting Midrashic passage [1] it is said: ". . . King Messiah, who has borne in himself sufferings and anguish for transgressors, as it is said (Isa. liii. 5): *He was wounded for our transgressions*—how much more will his sufferings be meritorious for all generations, as it is written: *The Lord hath laid on him the iniquity of us all* (Isa. liii. 6)." The interpretation thus differs among Jews as well as among Christians.

[1] The original MS. containing it is no longer extant, see Oesterley and Box, *The Religion and Worship of the Synagogue*, p. 96 (second edition).

But those who hold the view that the "Servant of the Lord" was an individual have a further question to ask themselves: Who was he? Was the prophet referring to some living person, or had he in mind some ideal personality? Here again opinions differ widely. When we have studied this Song we shall see to what conclusion we are led on this point.

Another preliminary point of much importance to be noted is that what, according to Deutero-Isaiah, is brought about by the direct act of God, is in these Ebed-Jahwe Songs described as being accomplished through the intermediary of the "Servant of the Lord." One illustration of this may be given. In xliii. 25 these words are put into the mouth of God:

I, even I, am He that blotteth out thy transgressions,
And I will not remember thy sins.

Whereas in liii. 5 it is said:

But he was wounded for our transgressions,
He was bruised for our iniquities,
The chastisement of our peace was upon him,
And by his stripes we are healed.

The fundamental contrast that is seen

here should be borne in mind throughout our study of lii. 13–liii. 12.

The translation to be given here is, as far as possible, that of the Revised Version; but in a number of cases the Hebrew text as we now have it is corrupt; where this is the case the translation is based on an emended Hebrew text. All the Ebed-Jahwe Songs are written in the same rhythmic style, as is indicated in the translation.

lii. 13. *Behold, my Servant shall prosper ; he shall rise,*
  He shall be lifted up and highly exalted ;
 14a. *As many were astonied at him (" thee " is a text corruption),*
  [*So shall he be glorious in the eyes of many*].

 15. *And he shall startle many nations,*
  Kings shall shut their mouths because of him ;
  For that which had not been told them shall they see,
  And that which they had not heard shall they consider.

These verses form a kind of introductory summary of the Song which has at the same time the object of riveting the attention by arousing expectancy as to what is going to come. It is not until the whole Song has been read that one apprehends the underlying sense of these verses.

The Hebrew of the word "prosper" means primarily "to be wise"; but the result of being wise is successfulness; and so the word has the secondary meaning, as here, of "being successful."[1] "He shall rise" adumbrates the Servant's life after death referred to later on in the Song; and the words which follow are a *résumé* of liii. 10–12. It will be noticed that as regards verse 14 only one line of the Revised Version occurs, and it is followed by a line which is not contained at all in the Hebrew, while two lines are missing; this requires some explanation. The whole of the Song, as already pointed out, so far as its outward form is concerned, is composed on a definite rhythmic pattern, viz. in a series of quatrains, or what in modern poetry we should call four-lined verses. The other three Ebed-Jahwe Songs are written on the same pattern. This being so dislocations and serious corruptions in the text are far more easily detected than would be the case

[1] See also Jer. xxiii 5: *He shall reign as king and prosper.*

with prose. Now verses 13 and 14 ought together to form one quatrain; there is, however, not only one line short, but something has been inserted which involves impossible grammar; this inserted matter consists of two lines, and both in form and subject-matter they quite obviously belong to the Song, *but not here*. If, however, these two lines [1] are taken away from their present context the quatrain is one line short, so that this has to be supplied conjecturally:

So shall he be glorious in the eyes of many.

We have put this in square brackets above (p. 88) to show that it does not correspond to anything in our present text; but that something of the kind stood there originally is extremely probable. This conjectural line is constructed on the basis of what appears to be a fragment of the original line left in the present text. As to the two lines which have got out of place, one cannot say for certainty where they belonged originally; but they come most

[1] They are enclosed within brackets in the Revised Version.

[2] The emendation of the text as above is that suggested by Duhm, *Das Buch Jesaia*, pp. 355 ff.

appropriately after liii. 2,[1] and we have inserted them there.

The meaning of the text as amended is much clearer; it is a summary of what is to follow: the Servant shall succeed in what he undertakes; he shall rise, and shall be greatly honoured; while, on the one hand, many were at first astonished at his mean and humble appearance, yet ultimately he will be glorified by many. It is quite possible that a redactor, reading the words, "As many were astonied at him," and thinking that the ordinary reader might not understand them, added here as an explanatory parenthesis the words which really came later on in the Song, and left them out of their proper place in order to avoid repetition.

iii. 1. *Who could have believed that which we have heard?*
And to whom hath the arm of Jahwe been revealed?
2a. *For he grew up before Him as a tender plant,*
And as a root out of dry ground.

So wonderful is that which has been

[1] This was first proposed by Marti, *Das Buch Jesaia*, p. 345.

divinely spoken to the ear of the prophet, so incomprehensible is God's purpose which has been revealed to the prophet, that it is not to be expected that ordinary men should believe it until it has actually come to pass before their eyes. And this is more especially so because the first beginnings of the working-out of this purpose seemed to be so insignificant and unimportant. He that is the great centre in the carrying-out of this purpose grew up in such obscurity, he appeared altogether so unworthy of notice, that He attracted no attention, men saw nothing special about him, or if they did it was to his detriment. This is further developed in the verse that follows :

> 2b. *He had no form nor comeliness,*
>   *Nor beauty that we should desire him ;*
> lii. 14b. *His visage was so marred, more than any man,*
>   *And his form more than the sons of men.*

The second line here is, in the Hebrew text, preceded by the word (it is only one word in Hebrew) " and when we see him," but the rhythm is spoiled by the insertion of it ; very likely it got into the text through its similarity with the word which follows.

One sees that lii. 14*b* comes in here most appropriately. The last line means that his form was so marred that it looked unhuman.

liii. 3. *He was despised and forsaken of men,*
A man of sorrows and acquainted with sickness;
And as one from whom men hide their faces;
Despised, and we took no account of him.

That concludes the description of the Servant's outward appearance. However difficult, or rather impossible, it may be to form any idea as to whom it was that the prophet referred, these lines force one to the conviction that it was an *individual* that he had in mind; to maintain that they are spoken in reference to the nation seems altogether unnatural.

4. *Yet it was our sicknesses that he bore,*
Our sorrows that he carried;
While we esteemed him stricken,
Smitten of God and humiliated.

The suffering of the innocent on behalf of others is seen already in 2 Sam. xxi. 1 ff., so that it is not *that* thought which is new here. In this latter passage we are told of seven men, belonging to Saul'' family, who were hanged on the mountain before the Lord as an atonement (2 Sam. xxi. 3) for Saul's treatment of the Gibeonites. These men, however, clearly suffered against their will. In the case of the Suffering Servant it is different; he accepts these sufferings *willingly*. And, moreover, as the text shows later on, God, Who lays these sufferings on him, does not do so because there is no other object upon which to vent His wrath, as it were; indeed, and this is a supremely important point, it is *not* on account of divine wrath for sin that the Servant undergoes this suffering; no, the object of the suffering, from the divine point of view, as well as from that of the Servant, is that it should be the means of *taking away* sin. The thought of punishment for sin is, no doubt, there; but punishment for sin does not *per se* obliterate sin; whereas the great object of the Servant's suffering is that sin should be *obliterated*. And this result it has, according to the teaching of this Song. The older conception of guilt entailing divine wrath venting itself in punishment, the idea of God avenging Himself for offences committed against

Him was a natural, and so far as it went, a fitting feeling, since it implied the sense of having done wrong and the feeling of penitence. But in this Song we enter an altogether more exalted spiritual sphere, and have (for the first time) the teaching that sin must be taken away by means of the voluntary acceptance of the results of sin by one man, a righteous man, on behalf of others:

5. *He was wounded* [1] *for our transgressions,*
   He was bruised for our iniquities,
   The chastisement of our peace was upon him,
   And through his stripes we were healed.

The thought-sequence must be conceived to be somewhat as follows: the existence of guilt is presupposed, it could not be otherwise; but it is not—at any rate not adequately—recognized and experienced by the guilty; therefore the stripes which were to have had the effect of making the guilty better and of removing the cause of sin were ineffective; thus new stripes and new blows became necessary; and, in consequence, "peace," i.e. the end of

[1] Literally, "he was pierced"; it is the same Hebrew word used in li 9 "Art not thou it . . . that *pierced* the dragon?"

God's punitive action (as it seemed to be) was impossible. All this is not explicitly expressed in the Song, but it seems to have been the thought-sequence behind it. Then God smote him who apprehended aright the reason of the stripes ; who realized that they were not an act of divine vengeance, but an ethical necessity ; and who, therefore, did not regard them as a misfortune which a man suffers because he must, but as a means of amelioration, and who voluntarily accepted them as leading to peace.[1] The phrase " the chastisement of our peace was upon him " means that the strokes dealt in order that they might be the means of making us right with God (the prophet is speaking in the name of the people) and thus bring about peace for us, were borne by him because their purpose was ineffective as far as we were concerned. " Peace " means spiritual wellbeing, brought about because the stripes are no more needed. Then there follows, not directly but by implication, the result that the lesson taught by the Suffering Servant has been learned by the people ; it is expressed by the further confession :

[1] Cp Duhm, *Op. cit.*, pp. 360 ff.

6. *All we like sheep have gone astray,*
   We have turned every one to his own way;
   And Jahwe hath caused to light on him,
   The iniquity of us all.

That confession means that there is a *spiritual* suffering on the part of the people, a suffering-together with the Servant, implying that they realize the reason for which the Servant suffers and that they themselves have now learned to suffer for the same reason; i.e. they have learned from the Servant that suffering is not the sign of divine wrath or vengeance, but that rightly borne it should be the means of taking away sin; in other words, that suffering is not an end in itself but a means.

Then the prophet describes the way in which the Servant bore his sufferings:

7. *Though oppressed, yet was he humble,*
   He opened not his mouth;
   As a lamb that is led to the slaughter,
   And as a sheep that before her shearers is
      dumb.

The words which follow, " Yea, he opened not his mouth," are tautologous after the mention of dumbness; they also overload the line and spoil the rhythm. It is most unlikely that they stood in the text originally. With this verse should be compared xlii. 2 in the first Ebed-Jahwe Song.

The next two verses speak further of his suffering and death, implying that it was a judicial murder ; yet it was for the wickedness of his people that he suffered death, while in him there was no sin. The text almost throughout the rest of the Song has suffered considerably through corruptions, and a good many emendations have to be made ; to go into detail on these points would involve an examination of the Hebrew text which would take us too far from our present purpose ; we must content ourselves with the results of such examination :

8. *From oppression and judgement he was taken away,*
And his place of rest—who considered it ?
For he was cut off from the land of the living ;
(Yet) for the transgression of the people was he stricken unto death.[1]

[1] " Stricken unto death " is the reading of the Septuagint,

9. *And they made his grave with the wicked*
   And with the godless [1] *his tomb ;* [2]
   Although he had done no violence,
   Neither was any deceit in his mouth.

Verse 10 is so corrupt that it is frankly untranslatable. A great many emendations have been suggested, and all necessarily involve much and drastic treatment of our present text. Of the large number we have considered that offered by C. J. Ball strikes us as breathing more than any other the spirit of the Song and as being most in harmony with its thought and teaching; he also bases his emendation as far as possible upon the very mutilated Hebrew text as we have it; for, after all, it is here that the original text is embedded. His rendering is as follows :

10. *But Jahwe was pleased to crush him ;*
    With sickness his soul was wasted ;
    But he saw a seed that would last,

---

[1] The Hebrew has " the rich ", but this has long been seen to be a corruption, it would be quite inappropriate here, and would not give the parallel with the preceding line which occurs so often in the Song.

[2] Literally, " his hill," i e sepulchral mound ; a very slight change in the text gives this reading which is a perfect parallel to " his grave " in the preceding line.

And Jahwe's purpose did prosper by his means.[1]

The text of the next verse is likewise very corrupt; based partly on the Septuagint it may be tentatively rendered thus:

11a. *He shall deliver his soul from travail,*
   He shall cause him to see light and be satisfied.[2]

Part of this verse has apparently fallen out at the beginning; the remainder belongs to the next quatrain:

11b. *My righteous Servant shall justify many,*
   For he bore their iniquities;
12a. *Therefore shall he inherit among the great,*
   And shall divide the spoil with the strong.

The last lines are easier as the text is better preserved:

12b. *For he poured out his soul unto death,*
   And was numbered with the transgressors;
   Yet he bare the sins of many,
   And made intercession for the transgressors.

The reward which is accorded to the Servant is the answer, in part, to the objection

---

[1] Quoted by Box, *Op. cit.*, p. 273.
[2] Cp. Psalm xxxvi. 8, 9.

which might be urged that an act of injustice seems to be done inasmuch as the Servant suffers bodily pain, though innocent, on behalf of those who are guilty, while these latter suffer, at the most, a spiritual pain. For the reward is very great; though he suffers death, the presumption thereby arising that all idea of reward is excluded, yet the wholly unexpected happens: he lives after death and receives the fulness of reward.

But the chief doctrinal importance of this Song is, firstly, the writer's recognition of the truth that sin involves suffering in one form or another; he is not concerned in giving a reason for this; he sees that that is the nature of sin; experience had taught him that it *is* so. Then as to the doctrine of Atonement which runs all through the Song, something wholly new is taught for the first time. Atonement for sin hitherto made consisted of animal sacrifices; but this spiritually-minded prophet presumably saw in the sacrificial system at the most an adumbration of some great truth. While it bore witness to the truth that there is such a thing as vicarious atonement, it (the sacrificial system) was wholly inadequate; it was inadequate because while a sacrifice could, according to the belief of the times, atone for a sin, it could do nothing to obliterate sin. It was a temporary expedient! Where there is vicarious atonement in any real sense the sufferer must not only suffer *willingly*, but he must know *why* he suffers, and must realize the good of it; and that can only be the case when the sufferer is a human being. The sacrificial system implied that God's wrath, aroused by sin, could be assuaged by bringing Him a sacrifice, i.e., that the suffering for sin which was the sinner's due could be transferred to an animal. The writer of these Songs taught that suffering which resulted from sin was not a sign of divine wrath, but a means of obliterating sin; and he presented a picture of one who illustrated this in his own person.

We saw, in speaking of these Songs above,[1] that while the present position of the first three Songs could be reasonably accounted for, this fourth one seemed to have nothing to do with its context; and that is undoubtedly so. But the main conceptions contained in it, and its composition, were due to the writer's realization of the fact that

[1] See pp 31 ff.

the doctrine of atonement underlying the whole sacrificial system was not only inadequate, but false; and not only so, but that that false doctrine of atonement involved of necessity also a false doctrine of God. This writer was not, it is true, the first to realize that the doctrine of atonement underlying the sacrificial system was derogatory to the honour of God, for an earlier thinker had said: *Will the Lord be pleased with thousands of rams, or with ten thousands of rivers of oil? shall I give my firstborn for my transgression, the fruit of my body for the sin of my soul* (Mic. vi. 7); and there were doubtless others after him who would say: *Thou delightest not in sacrifice; else would I give it thee; thou hast no pleasure in burnt offering. The sacrifices of God are a broken spirit; a broken and contrite heart, O God, thou wilt not despise* (Ps. li. 16, 17); or who would ask in the name of God: *Thinkest thou that I will eat bull's flesh and drink the blood of goats?* But the writer of this Song was the first to enunciate a new and really spiritual doctrine of atonement, which was far in advance of anything that had gone before. He taught with the object of abrogating the sacrificial system, and substituting for it a more spiritual means of relationship with God. In order to give concrete shape to his doctrine of Atonement, and to bring it home to his people in all its fulness, he constructed his picture of an *ideal personality*. Had his teaching been followed it would have meant the end of the sacrificial system, the beginning of a more spiritual worship and a deeper apprehension of God. But he was in advance of his times ; his teaching fell for the most part on deaf ears and blind eyes, and the benefit of it was reserved for later generations.

VI

THE DOCTRINAL STANDPOINT OF ISAIAH LVI.–LXVI

VI

THE DOCTRINAL STANDPOINT OF ISAIAH LVI.-LXVI

BEHIND these chapters there stands as the background an occurrence which, as a political event, was of insignificant importance when compared with the world-shaking events which form the historical background of Deutero-Isaiah; but as to the far-reaching and lasting effect of that occurrence it was beyond all comparison greater than the fall of kingdoms. To this occurrence we have already referred, but attention must again be called to it now. In B.C. 458 Ezra returned to Jerusalem with a certain number of the exiles; he came with the fixed purpose of teaching his people and impressing upon them *a new conception of the Law*, of which, as far as we know, he was the first great exponent. At first he does not seem to have been successful, at least, only in a moderate degree, but with the advent of Nehemiah in B.C. 445, things became different. Nehemiah came direct from the Persian court, armed with full powers to carry out what was required to be done in his own land. By building the walls of Jerusalem and being thus enabled to keep at a distance the country's foes, chiefly the mixed population of Samaria, Nehemiah accomplished a work of the greatest importance for Ezra, who was thereby able to carry out with success his original design. With enemies, who were such both politically and religiously, cleared out of the way, Ezra's task of inculcating the Law in accordance with his ideas and ideals became comparatively easy. By means of this the religion of the Jews received a new impress, a new character; not all at once, of course; but it became thereby the Judaism which, in the main, is the Judaism of to-day. There was, to be sure, a long struggle between the two main tendencies of thought, which grew more intense later on when Hellenistic influences came to bear upon the people, and when national, particularistic views were opposed by the freer and more expansive thought of those whose minds were impregnated with the Hellenistic spirit—a struggle which lasted right into New Testament times; but ultimately the movement initiated by Ezra triumphed, to the lasting detriment of Judaism. Nevertheless, we shall do well to remember that the new Judaism of which Ezra laid the foundation exercised a strong influence upon Christian thought and teaching, an influence which, in some respects, is probably as strong to-day as it ever has been. From the Christian point of view this is the most important result of the movement begun by Ezra.

Before we proceed it is necessary to observe that in Isaiah lvi.–lxvi. there are distinct indications that in some particulars the writer did not represent the attitude of vigorous insistence on legal observances and the extreme narrow prejudices which became characteristic in later times of the orthodox. We shall see in a moment some of the many signs of the rise of the new Judaism; but it is well to mention first one or two points which reveal a tolerant spirit and the view that there is something more important than the strict observance of the Law. Thus, it is taught that the mere fact of fasting is not enough; fast-days are good, but the spirit in which they are observed is what is really important; and, above all, there are things of greater moment than fasting : the passage in question is lviii. 3–7 ; it is well worth quoting in full :

" Wherefore have we fasted, and thou seest not ?
Wherefore afflicted ourselves, and thou takest
  no notice ? "
Behold, in the day of your fast ye find time for
  labour,
And ye exact all money lent on pledge [so
  amended text].
Behold, ye fast for strife and contention,
And to smite with the fist of wickedness.
Ye fast not this day (in such manner)
As to make your voice heard on high.
Is such the fast that I have chosen ?
The day for a man to afflict his soul ?
Is it to bow down his head like a rush,
And to spread sackcloth and ashes under him ?
Wilt thou call this a fast,
And an acceptable day to Jahwe ?
Is not this (rather) the fast that I choose :
To loose the bonds of wickedness,
To undo the bands of the yoke,
To let the oppressed go free,
And that thou break every yoke ?
Is it not to deal thy bread to the hungry,
And to bring the poor outcast to thy house ?
When thou seest the naked to cover him,
And not hide thyself from thine own flesh ?

The teaching that the command of the Law concerning fasting must be put aside in order that deeds of mercy may be accomplished is not that of the orthodox Judaism of later days. This is also true regarding the attitude of the writer towards non-Jews in such a passage, e.g., as lxv. i.:

I was enquired of them that asked not for me,
I was found of them that sought me not;
I said, " Here am I, here am I,"
To a nation that called not on my name.

Passages like these are exceptions, but it is right that they should be referred to before we come to our main subject, namely, the many indubitable indications in these chapters that the newer teaching which resulted from the activity of Ezra and his followers was beginning to take effect. The few examples that we shall consider (it would, of course, be impossible to deal exhaustively with this subject now) will be illustrated by some quotations from the authoritative writings which contain the teaching of later orthodox Judaism.

(1) *The Observance of the Law.*

At the very beginning of these chapters we hit upon two expressions the connotation of which agrees exactly with that which they have in later orthodox Judaism: " Keep judgement " means here " observe the law ";

and "do righteousness" means "do what is right according to the law." The context to which we shall come in a moment, fully bears this out. "Keep judgement"—"Do righteousness"; "by the first term is meant conformity to a system of ordinances, by the second a legal righteousness."[1] Nothing could be in more striking contrast than the different ways in which the writer of these chapters, and Deutero-Isaiah, respectively describe the means whereby the coming deliverance and salvation (upon which both writers lay great stress) is to be attained, i.e. the Messianic era. In the latter we have, for example, in lv. 1 these words:

Ho, every one that thirsteth, come ye to the waters !
And he that hath no money !
Come ye, buy and eat;
Yea, come, buy wine and milk without money and without price.

Here, in figurative language, the people are bidden to take what is *freely* offered them, namely the blessings of the Messianic era. Simple acceptation is all that is required.

Incline your ear, and come unto me;
Hear, and your soul shall live.

[1] Box, *The Book of Isaiah*, p. 286.

*And I will make an everlasting covenant with
    you,
Even the sure mercies of David* (lv. 3).

In lvi. 1, on the other hand, the coming salvation must be *acquired* by the fulfilment of legal ordinances : " Observe the law," i.e. do what is right in the way of legal ordinances. Nothing could be in more striking contrast than the points of view of the two writers on this point. We are reminded how in later times the gracious words were [spoken : " Come unto me, all ye that labour and are heavy laden, and I will give you rest " (Matthew xi. 28) ; while, on the other hand, St. Paul is constantly urging against the Jews the inefficacy of the righteousness which is by works of the law, e.g. Galatians ii. 16 f., and often in his epistle to the Romans.

That in the passage before us, lvi. 1 f., the reference is to the works of the law is quite clear from the context, and this leads us to our second point :

(2) *The Observance of the Sabbath.*

In lvi. 2 it is said :

*Blessed is the man who doeth this,
And the son of man that holdeth fast by it* :

*That keepeth the Sabbath from profaning it,
And that keepeth his hand from doing evil.*

And, again, two verses further on it continues:

*For thus saith Jahwe:
The eunuchs that keep my sabbaths,
And choose the things that please me,
And hold fast by my covenant;
Unto them will I give in my House, and within
    my walls, a monument and a name* [1]
*That is better than sons and daughters;
I will give them an everlasting name
That shall not be cut off.*

Now, it is worthy of note, firstly, that in Deutero-Isaiah the Sabbath is never mentioned; that again emphasizes the different point of view taken up here. Of course the Sabbath had been kept in earlier times, but in an entirely different way from that which was now taught; the change had taken place during the Exile and through Ezra's activity after the Return. The Sabbath and Circumcision had during the Captivity acquired the position of sacramental symbols of the religion of Jahwe as a result of the necessary cessation of the sacrificial system; these

---

[1] This line is too long in comparison with the rest; the words " and within my walls " are very likely an amplification added later, cp. Ps. cxxii. 7.

DOCTRINAL STANDPOINT OF LVI–LXVI

became the only two real marks of differentiation of the true Jew. The way in which the Sabbath observance of these later days differed from that of earlier times is referred to in lviii. 13 of our book:

If thou turn away thy foot from the Sabbath,[1]
Not doing thy pleasure on my holy day;
And callest the Sabbath a delight,
And the holy (day) of Jahwe honourable;
And if thou honour it, not doing thine own business,
Nor finding (therein) thine own pleasure, nor speaking thine own words;
Then shalt thou delight thyself in Jahwe,
And I will make thee to ride upon the high places of the earth;
And I will feed thee with the heritage of Jacob thy father;
For the mouth of Jahwe hath spoken it.

That is what one may call the newer, the "legal" way of observing the Sabbath. The difference between the old and the new, the pre-exilic and post-exilic, Sabbath has been well summarized thus: "Of the legal passages that speak of the Sabbath all those

[1] I e If the Sabbath is treated as something truly holy, like holy ground, cp. Exod. iii 5, if it is not *transgressed*.

which show affinity with the doctrine of the scribes—regarding the Sabbath as an arbitrary sign between Jahwe and Israel, entering into details as to particular acts that are forbidden, and by enforcing the observance by several penalties, so that it no longer has any religious value, but appears as a mere legal restraint—are post-exilic; the older laws only demand such cessation from daily toil, and especially from agricultural labour, as among all ancient peoples naturally accompanied a day set apart as a *religious festival*, and in particular lay weight on the fact that the Sabbath is a humane institution, a holiday for the labouring classes. As it stands in these ancient laws, the Sabbath is not at all the unique thing which it was made to be by the scribes " (*Encycl. Bibl.* iv. 4176). The passages quoted refer to the Sabbath just in the way described by these words; though in this particular case instead of enforcing its observance by penalties great rewards are offered, for it is said to him that keeps the Sabbath (the passage has already been cited):

Then shalt thou delight thyself in Jahwe,
And I will make thee to ride upon the high places
 of the earth;

*And I will feed thee with the heritage of Jacob
    thy father;
For the mouth of Jahwe hath spoken it* (lviii. 14).

That certainly approximates to the later Jewish ideas about the Sabbath, which as is well known, were of a very exaggerated character. It is maintained, for example, that the law of the Sabbath is equal to all the other laws and commandments of the Torah (*Shemoth R.* xxv.); and we notice that this section of our book opens with a blessing on those who keep the Sabbath; this is thus placed in the forefront:

*Thus saith Jahwe:
Keep ye judgement and do righteousness;
For my salvation is near to come,
And my righteousness to be revealed* . . .
    (lvi. 1, 2).

(3) *Almsgiving.*

We come next to the subject of *Almsgiving* under which is, of course, included deeds of mercy. The mention of this in the book is the most natural thing in the world; but the reason why attention is drawn to it is because of the close juxtaposition of good works and reward. Here are two examples; lviii. 7-9 (already quoted in another connexion):

Is it not to deal thy bread to the hungry,
And to bring the poor outcast to thy house?
When thou seest the naked to cover him,
And not hide thyself from thine own flesh?

Then follows immediately the reward:

Then shall thy light break forth as the morning,
And thy healing shall spring forth speedily,
And thy righteousness shall go before thee,
And the glory of Jahwe shall be thy rearward.
Then when thou criest Jahwe will answer,
When thou criest, He shall say: " Here am I " ...

Then, further, occur these words:

(And if) thou bestow thy bread on the hungry,[1]
And satisfiest the afflicted soul,
Then shall thy light arise in darkness,
And thy obscurity shall be as the noon-day,
And Jahwe shall guide thee continually,
And satisfy thy soul in dry places,
And thy bones will He make strong;
Thou shalt be like a watered garden,
And like a spring of water whose waters fail
not (lviii. 10, 11).

In such passages as these one sees the beginning of what in later Judaism developed into the doctrine of Works, namely that works are

[1] So the amended text.

meritorious and demand reward *per se*. But supreme among good works was Almsgiving which came to be called *Zedākāh* (צְדָקָה), "righteousness," because it was the pre-eminent righteous act. This is well illustrated by a Rabbinical comment on the words of Proverbs xxi. 3 (*To do justice and judgement is more acceptable to the Lord than sacrifice*), which says that he who gives *alms* (offers a sacrifice which) is greater than every sacrifice (*Sukkah* 49 *b*). It is taught that deeds of mercy and almsgiving are the means of acquiring justification in the sight of God, and therefore reward—reward, that is to say, not only in this life, but in the world to come. Indeed, it is taught again and again that *deeds of mercy and almsgiving gain eternal life for a man*.

The efficacy of works and the claim for reward is a doctrine which appeals to men as being no more than what bare justice demands ; and because that is true between man and man, it is also assumed to be true between man and God. In Judaism, where the doctrine of divine grace plays a relatively subordinate part this doctrine of the merit of works and the claim of reward is naturally very prominent. But it is just here where one of the fundamental differences between Judaism and Christianity lies. Christ put this most pointedly of all in His words : " When ye shall have done all the things that are commanded you "—the reference is obviously to the commandments of the Law—" say, we are unprofitable servants ; we have done that which it was our duty to do," i.e. nothing more ! It is unnecessary to recall how frequently St. Paul denies the efficacy of works alone, " lest man should glory." In the passages quoted just now from the third part of our book we have the mention together of works of mercy and almsgiving followed by the reward for these. It is not meant to say that when these words were written there was as yet any formulated doctrine on the subject such as is found in later Judaism ; but, as already pointed out, these chapters lvi.-lxvi. date from a time not very long after the return of Ezra from the Captivity, the time when a new conception of the Law—its paramount necessity, its extravagant claims, and the no less extravagant rewards for the fulfilment of those claims—when a new conception of the Law was coming into being ; it was a new era, epoch-making in the history of religion. These chapters date from

DOCTRINAL STANDPOINT OF LVI–LXVI

that time. In them, therefore, we have unmistakeable indications of the new trend of thought; they are only beginnings from which, in course of time, large developments grew. Their great importance, from a doctrinal point of view, is that they form one of our main sources from which to trace the growth and development of post-exilic Judaism; the form of Judaism, that is to say, which existed at the beginning of the Christian era, and which formed the background of early Christian teaching in many respects.

(4) *Superhuman beings.*

We come next to a subject of much interest, a subject which assumes considerable dimensions in later Judaism up to a certain point; and then we find that it was permitted to drop more and more into the background until it has now become to a great extent eliminated from Judaism; we refer to the belief in angels and superhuman beings intermediate *between God and men*.

In lxii. 6, 7, the prophet puts the following words into the mouth of God:

> *Over* [1] *thy walls, Jerusalem,*
> *Have I set watchers;*

---

[1] Not "upon" as in the Revised Version.

> *Neither day nor night*
> > *Do they hold their peace;*

then the prophet himself continues, addressing these watchers:

> *Ye that remind Jahwe,*
> > *Take ye no peace;*
> *And give Him no rest*
> > *Till He establish,*
> *Until He make Jerusalem*
> > *A praise in the earth.*

The "watchers" here mentioned are interpreted by some to refer to prophets; but this is not a term which is ever applied to them; and what these watchers do here—calling upon God day and night in order that the walls may be rebuilt—is not at all in the *rôle* of prophets; their duty is always to be active among the *people*, exhorting and warning, and turning them to God. Moreover, if prophets were here referred to would not our *prophet* himself be the first to remind God instead of calling upon others to do so? At any rate, he would have joined with them in doing this. And further, what we know of these times does not support the view that there were many prophets in existence, which would have to be the case if prophets are referred to in this passage. Although it is not definitely said so, it is evidently presupposed that these

DOCTRINAL STANDPOINT OF LVI–LXVI 123

watchers over the walls are many. Another reason against the view that prophets are referred to in these verses is that in verse 1 of this chapter the prophet himself says:

For Zion's sake I will not hold my peace,
And for Jerusalem's sake I will not rest,
Until her righteousness go forth as brightness,
And her salvation as a lamp that burneth.

That is the true *rôle* of a prophet, setting up righteousness among the people. So that it is very improbable that quite a few verses after the writer would impute to prophets such an entirely new *rôle*, in which he himself, moreover, takes no part. By the "watchers" are meant, not prophets, but heavenly messengers; so the early Jewish commentators on this passage interpreted the word. We find also that in the book of Zechariah, which belongs to this period, angels take a prominent part in carrying out God's will on earth. The mention of the "watchers" or angels shows that among the Jews there had arisen by this time belief in a heavenly hierarchy; this belief existed, it is true, in earlier times (as is proved by 1 Kings xxii. 19 ff.), but in a far less developed form. It was during the Exile, and under Babylonian influence, as we can see, for example, from the book of Ezekiel, that the developed belief in angels arose among the Jews. Its full development is seen in the Book of Enoch, where the angels are called, as in the passage we are considering, *watchers*. " And these are the names of the holy angels who watch " (Enoch xx. 1) ; [1] they are apparently called watchers because they do not sleep, for elsewhere in this book (*Similitudes* xxxix. 12, 13) it is said : " Those that sleep not bless Thee ; they stand before Thy glory and bless, laud, and extol, saying : Holy, holy, holy, is the Lord of Spirits ; He filleth the earth with spirits. And here my eyes saw all those who sleep not, how they stand before Him and bless, and say : Blessed be Thou, and blessed be the name of the Lord for ever and ever." It is obvious from this passage that those who sleep not, i.e. the watchers, refer to the angels. Of the activity of these the Book of Enoch constantly speaks ; it gives the names of many of them, and recognizes various grades in the angelic hierarchy. As to the names of the angels the Rabbis themselves say that they came from the Babylonians. In the passage under consideration (lxii. 6, 7) it will have been noticed

---

[1] The quotations are from Canon Charles' edition of the Book of Enoch

DOCTRINAL STANDPOINT OF LVI–LXVI 125

that the watchers, or angels, are represented as intercessors with God on behalf of men; it is interesting to note that the belief in this function of the angels became greatly developed in later Judaism. Already in the book of Tobit (xii. 15) we read that the angels present to God the prayers of the saints: " I am Raphael, one of the seven holy angels, who bear the prayers of the saints upwards . . ." In the book of Enoch the same thing is taught, as for example in liv. 1 : " I swear unto you, ye righteous, that the angels in heaven remember you for good in the presence of the glory of the Great One." And the same thing is to be found in other books both of the Apocrypha and Pseudepigrapha. It is also the teaching of the Rabbis; it is said, for example, that when Moses was exposed on the river, angels pleaded for him that he should not be allowed to perish (*Sota* 12*b*). In one of the Midrashic works (on Exodus xxi.) it is said that angels weave the prayers of men into crowns for the Most High. And, once more, it is taught in the Talmud (*Sukkah* 29 *a*) that interceding angels make it one of their duties to seek out the Jewish nation's special merits and to plead them in the presence of God. A special feature in the development of the doctrine of angels is the teaching that there are grades among them. Reference has already been made to the seven angels mentioned in the book of Tobit; ranks in the angelic hierarchy are spoken of or implied in many early Jewish works as well as in the later literature. An interesting passage in Philo runs: "The Father, the Creator of the Universe, gave to the archangel and most ancient Logos the privilege of standing on the confines separating the creature from the Creator, and of interceding between the immortal God and mortal man, as an ambassador sent from the ruler to the subject. *Rejoicing in this position, 'I stood between the Lord and you'* (Deut. v. 5), *being neither uncreated nor created, but between the two, pledge and security to the Creator and to the creature, a hope that the merciful God would not despise His work*" (quoted from *On one who is Heir* in the *Jewish Encyclopædia* I. 596a). This is written in reference to the archangel Michael, who occupies a very special position in the highest rank among the angels; he is spoken of in the pseudepigraphic literature as fulfilling the function of mediator; and in Rabbinical literature he is called the heavenly high-priest whose altar, upon which he offers

DOCTRINAL STANDPOINT OF LVI–LXVI

up sacrifices, stands in the fourth heaven. He is also described as the prince over all the angels, for he is the guardian-angel of the Israelite nation; he acts as Israel's representative and patron in the presence of God, and he intercedes there on behalf of his people; and the title given to him is that of the "Advocate of the Jews" (*Chagigah* 12 *b*). This developed angelology which became a characteristic of orthodox Judaism had its share in moulding, and ran parallel with, the conception of divine transcendence which was one aspect, as we have seen, of the Jewish doctrine of God; the teaching (of which the passage from Philo is an example) concerning semi-divine, superhuman beings who act as God's intermediaries, and are His agents in carrying out the divine will on earth is one which is not unconnected with this developed angelology. These semi-divine, superhuman beings are worth a passing mention here; for the beginnings of this belief are also to be seen in Isaiah lvi.–lxvi. These beings are the quasi-personification of certain attributes proper to God, and they occupy an intermediate position between personalities and abstractions. While on the one hand, they are represented as being so closely connected with God as to appear as parts of Him, or at all events attributes, they are, on the other hand, so often spoken of as undertaking individual action that they must be differentiated from God. They are: *Metatron*, or the next in rank to the divine ruler; the *Memra*, or the word of God; the *Shekhinah*, or the divine glory; and the *Holy Spirit*. The first three, though of much interest and importance, do not come into consideration in our book. But regarding the Holy Spirit a word must be said about the passage lxiii. 10 ff., which runs: "But they rebelled and grieved His holy Spirit . . ."; and a little further on there is mention of God having put His holy Spirit in the midst of the people. With the exception of Psalm li. 11 these are the only verses in the Old Testament in which the *holy* Spirit of God is spoken of.

Worthy of note is the expression "grieved the Holy Spirit,"[1] for this clearly supposes something coming very close to personality; the writer conceives of the Spirit as an independent being. This is precisely what is found to be the case in the teaching of later Judaism; in one place the Holy Spirit is

[1] Cp. Eph. iv. 30.

DOCTRINAL STANDPOINT OF LVI-LXVI

spoken of as the defender of Israel who enumerates before God the merits of the Israelites; elsewhere quotations from the Bible are referred to as the Holy Spirit's utterances, which accords with what is said in another passage that the Holy Spirit inspired men to write the books of the Bible. Numbers of other examples could be given, but these must suffice.

In this and the other points to which reference has been made—and other subjects as well which have not been touched upon—we have examples of the truth that Isaiah lvi.-lxvi. represents in a number of respects the beginning of the new Judaism of which the foundations were laid during the Exile and, above all, after the Return.

What was said at the commencement should, however, be repeated and emphasized once more, namely, that Isaiah lvi.-lxvi. presents, in addition to the type of Judaism which we have been considering, a wider and freer type; indeed, this latter is, of the two types, that which is more in evidence. But it has been with the narrower type of Judaism, of which these chapters contain so many elements, that we have been concerned, and this for two reasons; first, because, generally speaking, the commentaries do not give the prominence to this subject which it deserves ; and, secondly, because it is this type of Judaism which finally conquered. It is well to realize that the beginnings of this type of Judaism—which ultimately developed into Rabbinical Judaism—are very clearly to be discerned in these chapters.

VII

EXEGETICAL STUDIES

VII

EXEGETICAL STUDIES

In the large amount of material at one's disposal in these chapters it is not easy to choose out what passages should receive special attention. In a number of those selected, however, the object has been to illustrate the influence which this book has had on later thought among the Jews whether by expression or ideas. Other passages have been chosen because they are difficult; yet others because they seemed to offer some particular point of interest. But at the best they can only be few in number. For detailed exegesis of the book the bigger commentaries must be used.

As far as possible discussions on the Hebrew text have been avoided; but here and there it is quite indispensable to consider the original, otherwise the point in the exegesis is lost. But wherever possible we shall content ourselves with the text of the Revised Version.

xl. 3.

R.V. *The voice of one that crieth, " Prepare ye in the wilderness the way of the Lord . . ."*

R.V. (mg.) The voice of one that crieth in the wilderness, " Prepare ye the way of the the Lord. . . ."

There is no justification for the marginal rendering as far as the Hebrew is concerned. Possibly it was inserted in deference to the way in which the passage is quoted in the New Testament (Matt. iii. 3, Mark i. 3, Luke iii. 4, John i. 23); but this is taken from the Septuagint, not from the Hebrew. In the Septuagint the point of the passage is lost. But apart from that, the passage as quoted in the Gospels offers a good example of the way in which the Old Testament is sometimes quoted in the New Testament. When it is said in Matthew iii. 3, *This is he that was spoken of by Isaiah the prophet*, as though the prophet had foretold the coming of John the Baptist, the supposition is obviously wrong, as the context in Isaiah xl. shows. But the parallel between the words in the Septuagint,—*The voice of one crying in the wilderness*—and John the Baptist preaching in the wilderness of Judæa, seemed so strong that it was assumed that the earlier passage was a prophecy of the later one. A further step away from the meaning of the original was the use of the Vulgate rendering : *Vox clamantis in deserto*, which was quoted as an example of some one calling upon those who will not listen. This has come down to us in the phrase : " It is like someone preaching in the wilderness ! " where there is nobody.

The process was first to ignore the meaning of the words in the Old Testament, i.e., by the Septuagint, and then to ignore their meaning, in the New Testament.

But to return to the text again. The latter part of the verse runs : *Make straight* (or " level ") *in the desert a highway for our God.* The picture is here presented of God leading His people back from captivity to their own land upon this "highway." This word comes from a root (סלל) meaning to "cast up"; and this picture of constructing a highway, or causeway, is borrowed later by the writer of chapters lvi.–lxvi., e.g., in lvii. 14 : *Cast ye up, cast ye up, prepare the way, take up the stumbling-block out of the way of the people ;* lxii. 10 : *Cast up, cast up, the highway ; gather out the stones.* This is one example, of many, of the writer of lvi.–lxvi. using Deutero-Isaianic terms and phrases; and

people have pointed to these as a proof of
unity of authorship for both parts. Needless
to say, the argument is superficial. The
fundamental differences which prove that the
two parts cannot have been from the same
author, compel us to see in these similarities
the strong influence which the earlier writing
had upon the author of Isaiah lvi.-lxvi.

xl. 22.
He that sitteth above the circle of the earth,
So that the inhabitants thereof are as grass-
  hoppers ;
Who stretcheth out the heavens as gauze,
And spreadeth them out as a tent to dwell in.

In the third line some commentators would
follow the Septuagint and read : *Who stretcheth
out the heavens like a firmament;* but, as
Duhm points out, the heavens are not *like*
a firmament, but have been created such.
With this passage one must read Job xxii. 14 :

Thick clouds are a covering to Him that He
  seeth not,
And He walketh on the circuit of Heaven.

Somewhat *naive* as this conception is of God
dwelling above within a tent, as it were,
formed of thick clouds whereby He is shrouded
from view, in later Judaism the idea is

much developed, and there can be little doubt that passages like those before us formed the basis of future developments. Thus, it is taught that above the earth there are seven heavens; the highest of these, the seventh, is called *Araboth;* this is the dwelling-place (technically called *Mechıza*) of God. Not only does the Almighty dwell there, but the angels who serve Hım are there as well as the souls of the righteous.[1] Moreover, it is taught, there are three divisions in this "seventh heaven"; God Himself dwells ın the innermost division, which is hidden from view by a curtain (technically called *Pargôd*) of clouds; the righteous are in the next division, and the angels in the outermost. Behind the *Pargôd* of clouds where God dwells is the heavenly throne together with the "glory" of God.

It seems clear that these ideas have been developed from such passages as those quoted above.

xlıv. 3.

For I will pour water upon the thirsty (land), and streams upon the dry ground; and I will pour my spirit upon thy seed, and my blessing upon thıne offspring.

---

[1] Babylonıan Talmud,*Chagigah* 15b; for further detaıls see Weber, *Judische Theologıe*, pp 162 ff.

These words contain a twofold promise, namely, of material and spiritual blessings. But the special point of interest is the parallelism of the outpouring of water and of the spirit. By the spirit here is not meant a quasi-personality as in Isaiah lxiii. 10, but " spirit " in the sense of divine influence and power, resulting in well-being; as in the passage xxxii. 15, . . . *until the spirit be poured upon us from on high, and the wilderness become a fruitful field* . . . Nevertheless, the mention of water and spirit in the same context here is worthy of note ; the outpouring of the spirit completes that which is prepared by the outpouring of the water. The words remind us at once of some New Testament passages in which water and the spirit are mentioned in close connexion, e.g., John i. 31-33, iii. 5.

xliv. 6.

Thus saith the Lord, the King of Israel, and his redeemer, the Lord of hosts : I am the first, and I am the last; and beside me there is no God.

The title " King of Israel " (cp. xli. 21, " King of Jacob ") applied to God is found, as a formal title, here and in Zephaniah iii. 15

only. In other passages, almost exclusively in late books, God is spoken of as King; but this particular title "King of Israel" does not occur. The term "Redeemer" (Heb. גֹּאֵל), used in the English connotation, belongs in a special manner to Isaiah xl.–lxvi. Elsewhere it is the technical term for one whose duty it is to buy back a thing or a person; and especially is it applied to one who acts as an avenger of blood. In this sense, which is the older one, it does not occur in this book. The phrase "I am the first, and I am also the last" (cp. xli. 4, xlviii. 12, etc.) has an interest as being, almost certainly, the original source of the Christian formula A and Ω, "the beginning and the end" (Rev. xxi. 6, xxii. 13). Among the Jews the first and last letters of the Hebrew alphabet, א and ת, were used to express totality. Adam, it is said, sinned from א to ת, meaning that he was guilty of every sin. And again, it was said, that Abraham kept the Law from א to ת, meaning that he kept the whole Law. The Hebrew א and ת being a well-known formula expressive of entirety, was in all probability the prototype of the Christian A and Ω. In the Jerusalem Talmud (*Sanhedrin* i. 18*a*) Emeth, which means "truth," is said to be the name of God, Who includes all things; and the reason why this was the name of God was because it consisted of the first (א), middle (מ), and last (ת), letters of the Hebrew alphabet, thus including all things. In the Syriac New Testament *A* and *Ω* is rendered ܐܠܦ ܘܬܘ (= ת and א) the first and last letters of the Syriac alphabet—these two letters are the same as the Hebrew, though differently written. They are thus a formula expressive of God; and the idea contained in it, "the first and the last," is taken from this book (xliv. 6, xli. 4, xlviii. 12, etc.). So that it is in these passages that we see the origin of "I am Alpha and Omega, the beginning and the end,"—"the first and the last."

xliv. 8.
... Ye are my witnesses: Is there a God Or a Rock beside me at all?

The text of this verse is not in order, but with that we are not concerned just now. The point of interest centres in the title "Rock" used of God; "it designates Jahwe, by a forcible and expressive figure, as the unchangeable support or refuge of His servants; and is used with evident appropriateness where the thought is of God's unvarying attitude towards His people. The figure is, no doubt, like *crag, stronghold, high place*, etc. (Ps. xviii. 2), derived from the natural scenery of Palestine." [1] It is, however, possible that this title for God was originally borrowed from extraneous sources, for, according to Cheyne, " *Great Rock* (or mountain) is a common title of Assur and Bel in Assyrian." [2] However that may be, the title of " Rock " being given to God has a further interest for us on account of St. Paul's words in 1 Corinthians x. 1–4 : . . . *for they drank of a spiritual rock that followed them; and that rock was Christ.* The idea of the " spiritual rock " of which St. Paul here speaks would at first sight appear to have been derived from the rock mentioned in Numbers xx. 8 ff., out of which Moses brought forth water by striking it with his rod. But this is not so ; the curious haggadic legend to which St. Paul refers, and adapts, is seen, on reference to ancient post-biblical Jewish literature, to refer to the well spoken of in Numbers xxi. 16–18. In the Targum of Onkelos on this passage we

[1] Driver, *A Critical and Exegetical Commentary on Deuteronomy*, p. 350.
[2] Cheyne, on Psalm xviii. 2, quoted by Driver. In Deuteronomy xxxii. 31 " Rock " is used of a heathen deity.

read : " And from thence was given to them the living well, the well concerning which the Lord said to Moses, Assemble the people and give them water. Then, behold, Israel sang the thanksgiving of this song, at the time that the well which had been hidden was restored to them through the merit of Miriam . . . from the desert it was given to them for a gift. And from thence it was given to them in Mattanah ; turning, it went up with them to the high mountains, and from the high mountains it went down with them to the hills surrounding all the camp of Israel, and giving them drink, every one at the door of his tent." But how was it that this well came to be spoken of as a rock ? The answer is to be found in the Midrash Rabba on Numbers ; this is of much later date, but it contains many ancient elements. In its comment on Numbers i. 1 it says : " They had the well through the merit of Miriam, as it is written : ' And Miriam died, and was buried there.' And what follows immediately after ? ' And the congregation had no water.' And how was the well formed ? It was a crag like a beehive, and it use to roll along and accompany them on their journeyings. And when the standards were pitched, and the Tabernacle rested, the crag came and settled in the court of the Tent of Meeting, and the princes came and stood beside it, and said 'Spring up, O well,' and then it would spring up."[1]

St. Paul, in the Jewish manner which is so often to be observed in his writings, utilizes this old legend and makes the rock which was supposed to contain the well a type of Christ Who gives the living water. In speaking of that rock as Christ he was basing his words on Old Testament usage as illustrated in such a passage as that before us (cp. Hab. i. 12).

l. 10, 11.
Who is among you that feareth Jahwe?
Let him obey the voice of his servant.
He that walketh in darkness,
He that hath no light,
Let him trust in the name of Jahwe,
And stay upon his God.
Behold, all ye that kindle a fire,
That set alight firebrands:
Walk in the flame of your fire,
And among the brands which ye have kindled.
This shall ye have of mine hand,
Ye shall lie down in a place of torment.

These verses are added as an appendix to the third of the Ebed-Jahwe Songs.

[1] Quoted in Oesterley and Box, *Op. cit*, p. 97.

That they are a later addition is evident from the fact they reflect the cleavage *within* Israel after the time of Ezra; the law-abiding on the one hand and their oppressors and opponents on the other. The phrase " fearer of Jahwe " is a late technical expression for the faithful observers of the Law; like *Chassidim*. The eleventh verse describes the anti-Law party who by their subversive and destructive teaching are compared with such as kindle a fire. The Revised Version reads: " All ye that kindle a fire, that gird yourselves about with firebrands "; this last phrase is a little difficult, for it is not quite easy to see how anyone can gird himself with firebrands; a very slight emendation of the text, on the basis of the Septuagint and the Syriac, permits the rendering " that set alight firebrands," which is a more reasonable figure and affords a better parallelism with the first member of the verse. These men are bidden to walk in the flame of their fire, i.e., they are self-destructive. The words, " Ye shall lie down in sorrow," are not strong enough; they should be: " Ye shall lie down in a place of torment "; this, taken together with the immediately preceding reference to the fire in which these men shall walk, points quite clearly to Gehenna,—described in another late passage (lxvi. 24)—as a place where the worm does not die and the fire is not quenched. This is another indication that the verses under consideration are a later addition; for this Gehenna-conception is a great advance upon (and therefore belonging to a later period) the Sheol-conception which is the normal pre-exilic Israelite belief concerning the state of the departed beyond the grave.

li. 6.

Lift up your eyes to the heavens,
And look upon the earth (beneath);
For the heavens shall be torn asunder like smoke,
And the earth like a garment;
The [world] shall fade away, and its inhabitants
Shall die like gnats.
But my salvation shall be for ever,
And my " eternal welfare" shall not cease.

This rendering differs somewhat from the Revised Version, so a word or two of justification is demanded first. For the second clause the Revised Version renders: " For the heavens shall vanish away like smoke,

and the earth shall wax old like a garment."
The Hebrew word here translated "shall
vanish away" is נמלחו and occurs here
only in the Old Testament in the form of
a verb (it is a passive form, the Revised
Version makes it active); but as a noun
the root is found in Jeremiah xxxviii. 11,
12, where it means "rags," something
"torn asunder." It is, therefore, evidently
more correct to translate here "the heavens shall be torn asunder." The picture
is extremely realistic, being taken from
the ragged appearance of clouds when lashed
about by a high wind. The Revised Version continues: "and the earth shall wax
old as a garment"; but the verb here
belongs to the next clause; it is not wanted
here because the first verb "torn asunder"
applies to the heavens and the earth, and
is especially appropriate where the earth
is compared to a garment. Then the Revised Version goes on: "and they that
dwell therein shall die in like manner";
we have just seen that the verb in the previous clause belongs to this one, that verb
is תבלה, "shall fade away," but as the text
stands there is no subject to the verb;
now the whole, practically, of our book is

EXEGETICAL STUDIES

written in poetry, and in this clause the measure is too short, showing clearly that a word has fallen out of the text; the context makes it quite obvious what kind of word is wanting, for it says " the inhabitants thereof,"—whereof? Of course, of the world; the Hebrew word for " world " is תבל, which, excepting for one letter, has the same letters as the verb which precedes it, תבלה תבל; this similarity easily accounts for a scribe having inadvertently left it out in copying. Another point which goes to substantiate the correctness of this emendation is the fact that the word תבל is used of the *inhabited* world, as distinct from the earth (אֶרֶץ); in the text we have first mention of the destruction of the physical earth, then the reference to the world in the sense of the people dwelling on it. In the Revised Version it is said: " and they that dwell therein shall die in like manner," and that is literally what the Hebrew text reads (. . . כְּמוֹ־כֵן יְמוּתוּן); but the parallelism is feeble; we have doubtless here, too, a copyist's error, and a very excusable one, due again to the sameness of letters; he wrote as above instead of כְּמוֹ כִנִּים יְמוּתוּן (the letters ימ coming twice would easily be omitted once by mistake) meaning "like gnats." Then in the last clause the Revised Version renders: "but my salvation shall be for ever, and my righteousness shall not be abolished." "Righteousness" is, generally speaking, the right rendering of the Hebrew word צֶדֶק and צְדָקָה; but it is not always so. Here, for example, it stands parallel with "salvation," and has a meaning corresponding with this; we have rendered it "eternal welfare." It is the same in li. 1, 5, 8, where the reference is to that which righteousness has brought about, the *goal* of righteousness, in which is of course involved the idea of righteousness. Lastly, there is the word rendered in Revised Version "shall not be abolished"; this word in Hebrew is never used elswhere in this connexion; the Septuagint has οὐ μὴ ἐκλίπῃ (followed by the Vulgate) which presupposes לֹא תֶחְדָּל, "shall not cease."

So much for the justification of the rendering given above. One word as to the contents of the passage. The main thought which it contains is really very extraordinary considering the time at which it was written. That not only the things of the world, which day by day we see passing away before our eyes, are doomed, and that even the world itself is transient, but that in and above the world there is that which is eternal, namely, the glory and salvation that come of God's goodness in giving us religious belief; that is the greatest and most sublime thought that ever existed before the coming of Christ. Thus Duhm expresses himself in speaking of this passage; and assuredly he does not exaggerate. One recalls the words of Christ, "Heaven and earth shall pass away, but my words shall not pass away," and one realizes how much of great truth this prophet taught. The thought of the passing away of heaven and earth to which Deutero-Isaiah gives utterance here seems to have been the basis upon which in later days the expectation of a new heaven and a new earth was founded. This is expressed in lxv. 17 of our book: "Behold, I create new heavens and a new earth; and the former things shall not be remembered, nor come into mind," and again in lxvi. 22.

li. 9–11.
Rouse thee, rouse thee, put on strength,
 Arm of Jahwe!

Rouse thee as in days of old,
　As in ages of old time!
Art not thou he that clave in pieces Rahab,
　That pierced the Dragon?
Art not thou he that dried up the Sea,
　The waters of Tehom Rabbah?
That made the depths of the Sea a way
　For the redeemed to pass through?

This is one of the many passages in the Old Testament which refer to the ancient Creation-myth in which was described the conflict of Jahwe with Chaos, in the person of the Dragon, identical with Rahab. The Sea, which was regarded as the chaotic element in the ancient myth and was personified by Tehom Rabbah, the great deep (the Babylonian *Tiamat*), was subdued in this great conflict by Jahwe, but not finally destroyed. It is rather strange that in this passage (and the same occurs elsewhere in the Old Testament) the references to the myth of this primeval conflict are put on the same level with the historical fact of the passage of the Red Sea; both are assumed to be perfectly well known, since each is only alluded to, not described. Nothing could be clearer than that a belief was current among the people of Israel that in the distant past Jahwe had fought against and overcome Rahab, the Dragon, or Tehom Rabbah, and that this victory was regarded as evidence of Jahwe's power to overcome all the difficulties that stood in the way of the exiles' return. At the same time, one cannot but be surprised that a prophet who in general has such a high conception of God should, nevertheless, couple with it a belief involving such downright anthropomorphisms.

lvi. 4, 5.

... Unto them will I give in mine house and within my walls a memorial and a name
Better than sons and daughters;
I will give them an everlasting name,
That shall not be cut off.

The first line seems overweighted and probably the words " and within my walls " are an explanatory gloss. In the same line the word " memorial " involves an archæological note and will be spoken of later on.[1] The point of interest here is the mention of leaving a name by means of sons and daughters; it is true, the verse speaks of a means of leaving a name behind after

[1] See pp. 164 ff.

death which is better than that of having children to preserve it ; this latter, however, was the normal means. The desire " to possess a seed " finds frequent utterance in the Old Testament ; the reason, which often occurs in the later Psalms [1] and other books, was that the righteous might be rewarded after their death by having their memory preserved, and thus living on, as it were, after they had passed away. The desire of having one's name preserved is illustrated by a striking passage in Ecclesiasticus which is worth quoting in this connexion :

Have a care for thy name, for that abideth
    longer for thee
Than thousands of sparkling treasures ;
Life's goods last for limited days,
But the reward of a name for days beyond
    count.[2]

This thought of living on after death by means of one's name may well have prepared men's minds for, and thus have contributed towards, the belief in life after death in a fuller sense. Granted that it

---

[1] E g , Ps. xxv. 13 ; lxix 36 ; cii. 28 , cxii. 6, etc
[2] xli. 12, 13, according to the Hebrew.

was only the memory that was meant, still the name of the righteous departed continued to be a living thing, while at the same time the belief was present in the continuance of the existence, in however nebulous a form, of those whose memories were held in veneration. If one takes these two parallel thoughts, and contemplates them, is it not in the nature of things that, taken together, they should have formed one step upwards, at all events, in the development of the conceptions concerning the Hereafter ? [1]

lvii. 1, 2.

These verses belong closely to the preceding passage (lvi. 9-12) in which the iniquitous rulers of the people are described. In contrast to this the verses before us tell of the sad condition of the righteous. We get a picture here of the religious state of affairs as described in the books of Malachi, in parts of Ezra and Nehemiah, and in a number of the later Psalms. On the one hand, the self-seeking priesthood, on the other the " godly " or the " pious " who

[1] See the present writer's *Life, Death and Immortality : Studies in the Psalms*, pp 161 ff.

came to be known under the term *Chassidim* (almost the same word occurs here in verse 1, אַנְשֵׁי חֶסֶד "men of piety"), who in later days were represented by the Pharisaic party.

The rendering of the Revised Version is a little misleading in parts; the passage should be read as follows:—

The righteous man perished, and no man
    Laid it to heart;
And the men of piety were swept away,
    And no man took any heed.
For because of evil was the righteous man
    swept away;
    He entered into peace.
They lie upon their resting-places,
    (Every one) that walked uprightly.

The last four lines refer to the death which the righteous suffered on account of the prevalent evil. The phrase "entered into peace" as equivalent to death is striking; it shows the beginnings of the existence of a more advanced belief regarding the future life; it may be paralleled by the words in Job iii. 17:

There the wicked cease from troubling,
And the weary are at rest.

VIII

ARCHÆOLOGICAL AND OTHER
STUDIES

VIII

ARCHÆOLOGICAL AND OTHER STUDIES

THERE are a number of references in Isaiah xl.–lxvi. to religious and other customs which are of much interest. The meaning and significance of many of these references, though obvious enough to the people who heard or read the prophet's words, are not always clear to us at first sight, and need to be studied in the light of other sources before they can be properly understood. Some of these subjects will now engage our attention.

xliv. 5.

One shall say, " I am Jahwe's " ;
 And another shall call himself by the name of Jacob ;
While another shall inscribe upon his hand " Jahwe's,"
 And shall surname himself by the name of Israel.

These words occur in a passage describing Israel's glorious and peaceful future; so happy will this be for Israel under the gracious guidance and protection of Jahwe that many from among the heathen nations will come and declare their allegiance to Him by joining themselves to the nation of Israel. But the passage has been chosen on account of the point of archæological interest contained in the third line. The Revised Version renders this: "And another shall subscribe with his hand unto the Lord"; this is misleading; but the margin renders more correctly: "shall write on his hand, Unto the Lord"; though even this is not quite what the original implies, which is rather this: "shall inscribe upon his hand 'Jahwe's.'"[1] This may be paralleled by what one finds inscribed on many seals which have been found in Palestine, belonging to many different ages; most of these are inscribed with the name of the possessor, e.g. "Shebaniah's"; very often the name of the possessor's father is added: "Son of . . ." Every seal thus marked denoted ownership. In the same way, in the passage before us, a man marked

[1] See also Isa. xlix. 16.

himself with the name of Jahwe to show that he belonged to Jahwe; and this is to be understood in a literal sense, for the reference is to the custom of imprinting marks on the person in sign of consecration to a deity. Such a tattooed mark meant that the person in question belonged to the god whose sign he thus bore. There is plenty of evidence that this custom was widely prevalent among Semitic peoples in ancient times; one of the most striking pieces of evidence is that of Lucian in his *De Dea Syria*, lix.: "They all tattoo themselves—some on the hands and some on the neck—and so it comes that all the Assyrians bear stigmata." That the custom was practised by the Israelites is seen by Leviticus xix. 28 (cp. Lev. xxi. 5), where tattooing is condemned as a heathenish practice. As Robertson Smith points out, in this passage in Leviticus the practice "is immediately associated with incisions in the flesh made in mourning or in honour of the dead, and this suggests that in their ultimate origin the *stigmata* are nothing more than the permanent scars of punctures made to draw blood for a ceremony of self-dedication to the Deity" (*The Religion of the Semites*, p. 334, cp. *Kinship*, pp. 249 ff.).

The subject of these marks upon the body recalls an interesting passage in the Old Testament from which it is to be gathered that the prophets of Israel, or at least the earlier ones, were distinguished by a special mark, either a tattoo or a cut of some kind, on the forehead. In the passage in question (1 Kings xx. 35–43) a certain prophet is sent to rebuke king Ahab for having permitted Benhadad, king of Syria, to go free after his defeat, and for having made a covenant with him, instead of preventing him from injuring Israel, at some later date, by imprisoning him or putting him to death. The prophet delivers his message in the form of a realistic parable. In order to present himself before king Ahab as one who had been in the battle, he asks a fellow-prophet to wound him; on the latter refusing he gets another man to do so. Then the prophet, with the would-be marks of battle upon him, waits for the king to pass by. But fearing lest the king should not listen to the words which the prophet feels called upon to speak to him, if he knew that this speaker was a prophet, he disguises himself with "a headband over his eyes." The king comes; then the disguised prophet addresses him, saying that during the battle a prisoner had been entrusted to his care, and that he had staked his life on the safe custody of this prisoner; but that the latter had escaped. The king is in no doubt as to what the consequence must be—his life is forfeit. Then the prophet suddenly snatches the headband from his forehead, and immediately the king "discerned that he was one of the prophets." The prophet then delivers his message: *Thus saith the Lord, Because thou hast let go out of thy hand the man whom I had devoted to destruction, therefore thy life shall go for his life, and thy people for his people.*

It seems clear from this account that there was some distinguishing mark whereby a prophet could be at once recognized. If it stood alone it would be precarious to build too much upon it; but there are other indications which point in the same direction. There is, in the first place, the analogy of circumcision; if the *people* of Jahwe had a distinguishing mark in token of their belonging to Him (see Gen. xvii. 11; xxi. 4), there would be nothing strange if

another distinctive sign should mark Jahwe's prophets who were in a more intensive manner Jahwe's people. In the second place, in addition to various passages [1] which refer to bodily marks, showing that the custom was in existence among the Israelites for one purpose or another, we have in Zechariah xiii. 4–6 the direct statement that the prophets had a prophetical mark, not, it is true, on the forehead, but on the hands:
And it shall come to pass in that day, that the prophets shall be ashamed every one of his vision, when he prophesieth; neither shall they wear a hairy mantle to deceive; but he shall say, I am no prophet, I am a tiller of the ground; for I have been made a bondman from my youth. And one shall say unto him, What are these wounds between thy hands? Then he shall answer, Those with which I was wounded in the house of my friends.

Lastly, it is perhaps not fanciful to see an analogy in the custom, evidently well known in early Israel, of putting a mark

---

[1] Very possibly one of these is 2 Kings ii. 23, where the prophet Elisha's baldness is spoken of, this baldness may have been a prophetic mark, for the same word is used of a mark between the eyes in Deut xiv 1, though in this last passage the cutting was a mark of mourning.

on cattle to denote ownership; just as the owners of herds marked them as their property, so the people of Jahwe were marked to show that they belonged to him; and, in the case of the prophets, there would be a special mark.

xlvii. 13.

Thou art wearied with the multitude of thy counsellors,
  Let them now stand forth
And save thee: the astrologers,
  And they that gaze at the stars,
And they who foretell month by month
  The things that shall come to pass.

Here we have reference to astrologers, star-gazers, and monthly prognosticators. The prophet, who is prophesying the impending fall of Babylon, mockingly calls upon the Babylonians to seek the help of their astrologers to avert the coming catastrophe. Three expressions are used: For the word rendered in the Revised Version "astrologers" the Hebrew has "dividers of the heavens"; the reference is to the division of the heavens into the twelve "stations" of the Zodiac; these "stations" are spoken of in 2 Kings xxiii. 5

as among the things to which the Israelites burned incense. The fate of the nation, as well as of individuals, was supposed to be indicated by the relative conjunction of the sun, moon and the five planets, with the signs of the Zodiac. The next expression, "star-gazers," (lit. "gazers into the stars") merely describes the method of the astrologers; while the third, rendered in the Revised Version "prognosticators," is more literally "those who make known at the new moons"; the reference "seems to be to the official reports drawn up by the Babylonian astrologers to be sent to the king month by month. Many such Assyrian reports are still extant, and one of them gives us an astrological calendar, each month or day of which is noted as being lucky or unlucky for the commencement of a campaign, or for other operations" (*Encyclopædia Biblica*, iv. 4785).

lvi. 4, 5.

. . . Unto them will I give in mine house and
  within my walls a memorial and a name
Better than sons and daughters;
I will give them an everlasting name,
That shall not be cut off.

We have already considered this passage

in another connexion;[1] here we shall deal with a small point which has some archæological interest. From the context it will be noticed that the reward described in the words quoted above is promised to certain men who "keep my sabbaths, and choose the things that please me, and hold fast by my covenant." For these there is to be a "memorial" in God's house, i.e. in the Temple. The Hebrew word for "memorial" here means literally a "hand"; it is used in the technical sense of a memorial or "monument" in 1 Sam. xv. 12 of Saul setting up a monument in Carmel; and in 2 Sam. xviii. 18 there is the following note which must be read in connexion with the passage before us: *Now Absalom in his lifetime had taken and reared up for himself the pillar, which is in the king's dale; for he said, I have no son to keep my name in remembrance; and he called the pillar after his own name. And it is called Absalom's monument* (lit. "hand") *unto this day*. There is no doubt that the reason why such a monument was called a "hand" was because on the pillar a human hand was depicted; examples of this are in

[1] See pp. 151 ff.

existence.[1] As to what the meaning of this was there is diversity of opinion; some think that it was in token of the person commemorated being a true member of the community; others that it denoted a beckoning hand inviting the passer-by to remember the name of the one commemorated; others, again, believe that it signified the hand raised when taking the oath of fealty to the Deity; in the passage before us this would apply to the oath made to keep the covenant mentioned in the text. The last explanation would appear to be the most probable. But the question is a difficult and complicated one.

However, this very ancient custom among the Jews of setting up memorials of saintly men in the house of God has been adopted and continued ever since.[2]

lvii. 3-9.

. . . . .

5. *Ye that enflame yourselves among the oaks,*
   And under every green tree;
That slay the children in the valleys,
   In the clefts of the rocks.

[1] See, e g. Robertson Smith, *The Religion of the Semites*, p. 457.
[2] See Kohler in the *Jewish Encyclopædia*, iii 671b.

6. *Among the smooth stones of the valley is
    thy portion;
    They, they are thy lot;
    Even to them hast thou poured a drink-
      offering,
    Thou hast offered an oblation.
    [Shall I be appeased for these things?]*
7. *Upon a high and lofty mountain
      Hast thou set thy bed;
    Thither also wentest thou up
      To offer sacrifice.*
8. *And behind the doors and the posts,
    Hast thou set up thy memorial.*

. . . . .

9. *And thou wentest to the king with ointment,
    And didst increase thy perfumes;
    And didst send thine ambassadors afar off,
    And didst debase thyself to Sheol.*

In this passage there are several points worth touching upon. The words are spoken in reference to the practices of the mixed population which, as we learn from the books of Ezra and Nehemiah, was such a thorn in the side of the Law-observing followers of Ezra. The prophet inveighs against the religious customs and worship of these semi-Israelites which constituted a grave danger to the purer monotheistic worship of the returned exiles.

He speaks of their impure and cruel rites, the offering-up of children in sacrifice, and of their sacrificing to idols; these are the things which were practised in Israel long previously; they are described in 2 Kings xvii., where it is said that owing to them the northern kingdom had been carried away captive into Assyria. One or two of the references to these customs in the passage before us are a little obscure. In verse 6 there is mention of "smooth stones of the valley" to which drink-offerings are poured. By these "smooth stones" are meant boulders of unhewn stone which, according to ancient custom, were used for altars (see Exod. xx. 25, *And if thou make me an altar of stone thou shalt not build it of hewn stones; for if thou lift up thy tool against it, thou hast polluted it*; cp. Deut. xxvii. 5, 6). Such stones would be found in valleys smoothed by the action of the water of the winter torrents. The true Jahwe worshippers had chosen Him as their "portion," as it is expressed in various Old Testament passages (Ps. xvi. 5, *Jahwe is the portion of mine inheritance*, cp. Deut. iv. 19; Jer. x. 16), instead of this these people had chosen as their portion these smooth stones.

ARCHÆOLOGICAL STUDIES 169

In the Hebrew there is a striking word-play here:

בַּחַלְקֵי־נַחַל חֶלְקֵךְ:

The way in which the drink-offerings were poured upon these stones has been illustrated in an interesting way thanks to recent excavations in Palestine.[1] The last words in verse 6, *Shall I be appeased for these things?* are so entirely out of place that they cannot have formed part of the original text; they are probably a corrupt marginal note which the Septuagint read in its correct form: " Shall I not therefore be provoked to wrath for these things ? " In the following verse the well-known worship on the hill-tops is mentioned; this, together with the preceding, were the public forms of worship held out of doors by the people already referred to. Verse 8 speaks of the signs of heathen customs in the houses, *behind the doors and the posts hast thou set up thy memorial.*[2] As to what this actually was there is some difference of opinion; but we need not go into the question. In verse 9: *And thou wentest to the king with ointment* . . . the reference

[1] See the *Quarterly Statement* of the Palestine Exploration Fund, 1903, p 27.
[2] Cp. the *Mezuzah* or Door-post Symbol found in the houses of all orthodox Jews at the present day.

is to the Ammonite deity Melek (the Hebrew word for king), generally vocalized Milkom in the Massoretic text. The last words of this verse, *and didst debase thyself to Sheol*, refer to those who went to consult oracles in underground places of worship dedicated to subterranean deities. From the words, *thou didst send thine ambassadors far off*, it is clear that messengers were sent far afield to inquire of the gods of other countries; this was often done by the peoples of antiquity.

lxv. 1-5; *lxvi.* 17.

1. *I was inquired of them that asked not for me* . . .
2. *I have spread out my hands all the day*
    To a rebellious people;
    Which walketh in a way that is not good,
        After their own thoughts;
3. *To a people that provoketh me*
        To my face continually;
    That sacrifice in gardens,
        That burn incense upon bricks,
4. *That sit among the graves,*
        And spend the night in vaults;
    That eat swine's flesh,
        And broth of abominable things is in their vessels;
5. *Which say, " Stand off,*
        Come not near me lest I sanctify thee ! " . . .

ARCHÆOLOGICAL STUDIES 171

The reference is again to the practices of the mixed population of Palestine among whom heathen rites were practised. Many of these rites went back in their origin to a hoary antiquity; there are some interesting points about them which are worth discussing.

That sacrifice in gardens. In Isaiah xvii. 10, 11, in the " Oracle concerning Damascus," it is said, according to the Revised Version :

. . . Therefore thou plantest pleasant plants,
And settest it with strange slips ;
In the day of thy planting thou hedgest it in,
And in the morning thou makest thy seed to blossom ;
But the harvest fleeth away in the day of grief,
And of desperate sorrow.

In the first line " pleasant plants " should be, as the margin of the Revised Version renders it, " plantings of Adonis." In the third line " thou hedgest it in " should be " thou makest it to shoot up," or something similar; the Hebrew word has this sense as well. And in the last line but one " the harvest fleeth away " is explained in the margin of the Revised Version by the rendering, " the harvest shall be a heap," i.e. of rubbish. The meaning is that the plant very soon grows up and very soon withers.

The reference in this passage, as well as in lxv. 3 where the "sacrificing in gardens" is spoken of, is to the so-called "gardens of Adonis" which are mentioned by a number of ancient authors. "These were baskets or pots filled with earth, in which wheat, barley, lettuces, fennel and various kinds of flowers were sown and tended for eight days, chiefly or exclusively by women. Fostered by the sun's heat, the plants shot up rapidly, but having no root they withered as rapidly away, and at the end of eight days were carried out with the images of the dead Adonis, and flung with them into the sea or into springs. These gardens of Adonis are most naturally interpreted as representatives of Adonis or manifestations of his power; they represented him, true to his original nature, in vegetable form, while the images of him, with which they were carried out and cast into the water, portrayed him in his later human form. All these Adonis ceremonies, if I am right, were originally intended as charms to promote the growth or revival of vegetation; and the principle by which they were supposed to produce this effect was homœopathic or imitative magic. For ignorant people suppose that by mimicking the effect which they desire to produce they actually help to produce it; thus by sprinkling water they make rain, by lighting a fire they make sunshine, and so on. Similarly, by mimicking the growth of crops they hope to ensure a good harvest. The rapid growth of the wheat and barley in the gardens of Adonis was intended to make the corn shoot up; and the throwing of the gardens and of the images into the water was a charm to secure a due supply of fertilizing rain."[1] It is against some form of this rite, connected as it was with a heathen deity, that the prophet inveighed; see further below on lxvi. 17 (p. 176).

That burn incense upon bricks. It is not easy to understand what is referred to by this practice, nor why it was regarded as objectionable. We know, however, that bricks were made of sun-dried clay and it is quite possible that the reference is to the burning of incense on small altars made of clay. That this is what is meant is the more likely inasmuch as such a clay incense-

---

[1] Frazer, *The Golden Bough; Adonis, Attis, Osiris*, pp. 194 f. (1907). Cp. also Lagrange, *Études sur les Religions Sémitiques*, pp. 173 ff.

altar was discovered not long ago by Dr. Sellin on the site of ancient Taanach, lying to the west of Mount Gilboa in the north of Palestine; the decorations on this little altar would fully explain why the prophet inveighed against the use of such things. It was a four-sided vessel of baked clay, about three feet high; there was no bottom to it, but on the front of it at the base were two small holes; on each of the sides there were four holes, rather larger, and at the back was a somewhat larger opening. The method of procedure was the same as that of an ordinary oriental oven; the fire was lighted on the ground, and the vessel placed over it; sufficient draught was secured by the way in which the holes were made; and the incense was placed in a receptacle made for it at the top. The decorations consist of three winged figures with the head of a man and the body of a beast; these are on either side of the altar; on the front of it there is the representation of a figure in conflict with a great serpent. Below this mythological picture is another; a tree having a goat on either side with its head turned towards the tree. It cannot be doubted that the presence of these figures points to some form of worship other than or in addition to, that of Jahwe. So that if this incense-altar is in any way connected with the practice referred to in our passage as "burning incense upon bricks," one can understand the prophet's objection to it as it was a violation of the monotheism upon which he naturally lays so much stress.

That sit among the graves, and spend the night in vaults. The reference here is to the practice of seeking an oracle from the dead. This is referred to in Isaiah viii. 19, where the prophet speaks of those who say: *Seek unto them that have familiar spirits and unto the wizards, that chirp and mutter; Should not a people seek unto their God? On behalf of the living should they seek unto the dead?* See also xxviii. 15; 2 Kings xxi. 6. The object was to obtain knowledge, as was believed, of the future; this we learn from the most striking passage on the subject in the Old Testament, 1 Samuel xxviii. 7-21. With this last passage (the witch of Endor episode) we cannot concern ourselves here; but from Isaiah viii. 19 it is easy to see that the wizards resorted to impudent chicanery; for, by means of what may have been a species of ventriloquism, they pretended to receive communications from the departed. The *rendez-vous* at night (this is implied by the Hebrew word, though not expressed in the Revised Version) at grave-sides or in rock-hewn vaults was well calculated to arouse the superstitious expectations of the dupes.

That eat swine's flesh, and broth of abominable things is in their vessels. With this passage we must read lxvi. 17 :

They that sanctify and purify themselves
　For the gardens behind the one in the centre,
That eat swine's flesh,
And creeping things, and the mouse . . .

To deal first with this last passage ; the two first lines refer to the mystery rites in which a central initiated person took the lead ; ablutions and the like were preparatory to the religious exercises which took place in the gardens of Adonis, already referred to. In the last line " creeping things " [1] is a rendering based on a slight emendation of the Hebrew in accordance with Leviticus xi. 29 ff., where it says : *And these are they which are unclean unto you among the creeping things that creep*

---

[1] The Revised Version renders " the abomination."

ARCHÆOLOGICAL STUDIES 177

upon the earth; the weasel and the mouse and the great lizard after its kind. . . . In another passage, Isaiah lxvi. 3, the swine is again spoken of, and mention is also made of the dog as an unclean animal which was sacrificed. In regard to all these and similar passages in the Old Testament, Robertson Smith says: "All these passages refer to the same circle of rites, in which the victims chosen were such animals as were strictly taboo in ordinary life—the swine, the dog, the mouse and vermin generally. To such sacrifices, as we learn from Isaiah lxvi. 17, a peculiar consecrating and purifying efficacy was attached, which must be ascribed to the sacramental participation in the sacrosanct flesh.[1] The flesh was eaten in the form of broth which in lxv. 4 is called broth of *piggūlīm*, i.e. of carrion, or flesh so killed as to retain the blood in it (Ezek. iv. 14; cp. Zech. ix. 7). We are to think, therefore, of a broth made with the blood, like the black broth of the Spartans, which seems also to have been originally a sacred

[1] Robertson Smith thus connects the purifying and sanctifying, spoken of in lxvi. 17, with the sacrificing and partaking of these animals; we are, however, convinced that the two rites were entirely distinct The prophet, as in lxv 1–5, is enumerating a whole series of heathen practices which are not necessarily connected.

food, reserved for warriors. The dog-sacrifice in lxvi. 3 is killed by breaking its neck, which agrees with this conclusion." [1]

Which say, " Stand off ; come not near lest I sanctify thee." This passage, as pointed out by Duhm, is to be understood in the light of Ezekiel xliv. 19 : *And when they go forth into the outer court, even into the outer court of the people, they shall put off their garments wherein they minister, and lay them in the holy chambers, and they shall put on other garments, that they sanctify not the people with their garments.* Just as the priests here mentioned had to take care that the people should not come in contact with their holy garments lest the people should become " sanctified," so the heathen mystic, in the passage under consideration, had to warn the worshippers not to come near him lest they should be " sanctified " by the atmosphere impregnated with magic charm which surrounded him.[2] The matter may be explained somewhat in this way : To man in a more or less low state of culture and religion the distinction between the conceptions of what we speak of as holiness and uncleanness does not exist ; but

[1] *Religion of the Semites*, p. 343.
[2] Cp. Elijah's magic mantle in 2 Kings ii. 14 (Duhm).

as soon as a higher form of religion develops a distinction begins to be discerned. Thus, in the lower stage a dead body, for example, would be regarded as "holy," i.e. something to be kept separate [1] and avoided because it was thought of as being possessed by evil spirits; a medicine man's belongings would be regarded as "holy," i.e. something to be kept separate and avoided, because they partook of the "holiness" of the medicine man who was looked upon as a "holy man." Both the dead body and the medicine man's belongings are uncanny things inspiring mysterious fear; both impart a supernatural infection and are therefore dangerous. It is this which, to the mind of man in a low stage of culture, puts both in the same category. With the rise of a higher religion the dead body would come to be regarded as "unclean," while a priest's vestments (corresponding in some sense, for the purposes of our present argument, to the medicine man's utensils) would come to be regarded as "holy." But, and this is the important point, both would still be avoided; the former because contact with it involved pollution, the latter because a certain indefinable holiness ad-

[1] The Hebrew word for "holy" connotes "separateness."

hered to it. In the case before us the performer of the mystic rites (himself immune, of course, because he is a qualified agent) warns the worshippers not to come near him because of the conviction that harm would come to them if they were infected by the divine, or demonic, atmosphere in which he stood.

* * *

The above are only a few of the many passages of archæological interest which occur not only in Isaiah xl.-lxvi., but throughout the book of Isaiah. They have been chosen because they well illustrate many of the beliefs and superstitions which had to be shaken off before a purer form of religion could become dominant among the Jewish people. The task which lay before the prophets and teachers of this period was of profound difficulty ; but they succeeded ; and it is difficult to see how they could have succeeded unless it had been by means of putting the Law and its manifold observances before the people as a set-off against the religious activities of a low and revolting character, in many respects. The Law kept them busy and occupied their minds with better things ; and this, failing the best things, for which the people were not yet prepared, was very good.

INDEX

Ablutions, 176
Abraham, 139
Absalom's monument, 165
Activity of angels, belief in, 79
Adonai, 27
Adonis, plantings of, 171
Advocate of the Jews, 127
Ahab, 160
Aleph to Tau, 139
Alexander, 8
Alliterations, 9
Alms greater than sacrifice, 119
Almsgiving, 117 ff
Alpha and Omega, 139 f
Altar of clay, 173 f
Altars of unhewn stone, 168
Ammonite deity, 169
Ammonites, 59
Angel, guardian, 127
Angelic beings, 78 f, 122 ff
Angels, grades among the, 126
—, names of from Babylonia, 124
—, intercessors, 125
Animal sacrifices, 101
Anthropomorphic conceptions, 74
Anthropomorphisms, 82, 150
Apocalyptic passages in Isaiah, 9
Arabians, 59
Araboth, 137
Armenians, 61
Assur, 141
Assyria, 53, 168
Assyrian colonists, 58
Assyrians, 159
Astrologers, 163
Astyages, 56
Atonement, 56, 74, 101
—, doctrine of, 69 ff, 85 ff.
—, false doctrine of, 103
—, later Jewish teaching on, 71
—, spiritual doctrine of, 103
—, through chastisement, 71
—, through suffering, 70
—, vicarious, 101 f
Avenger of blood, 139

Babylon, 28, 51, 52, 57, 62, 163
—, downfall of, 5
—, exiles in, 54 ff
Babylonian exile, 50

Babylonian influence, 123
Babylonians, 61
Badge of prophet, 160
Baldness of Elisha, 162
Beings, superhuman, 121
Bel, 141
Beliefs, superstitious, 180
Benhadad, 160
Biblical books, dates of, 49
— books, editing of, 56
— quotations utterances of the Holy Spirit, 129
Blood, avenger of, 139
Bricks, 173
Broth, 177

Canaan, language of, 8
Captives, enumeration of returned, 50
Captivity, no sacrifices during, 72
Chassidim, 144, 154
Chastisement, 96
—, a means of atonement, 71
Chaos, 150
Christ, dual nature of, 82
Christian doctrine, influence of Judaism on, 46
Christianity, difference between Judaism and, 120
Circumcision, 56, 114
Clay altar, 173 f
Colonists, Assyrian, 58
Commentators, Jewish, 123
Conjectural emendation of Hebrew text, 90
Consecration to a deity, 159
Corruption in Hebrew text, 72, 88, 89 ff., 99, 147
Creation-myth, 150
Crœsus, 57
Cyrus, 29, 35, 36, 56
—, God's instrument, 57

Damascus, 171
Darius, 61
Dates of Biblical books, 49
Day of the Lord, the, 62
Dead Sea, 59
Debt, payment of, 70
Deity, consecration to, 159
Deutero-Isaiah, idealism of, 29 ff.

INDEX

Deuteronomy, book of, 56
Distinguishing marks of Jews, 56
Dividers of the heavens, 163
Divine grace, 73, 119
— love, 73
Doctrinal Standpoint of Isaiah xl–lv, 67 ff
— — —, lvi–lxvi, 107 ff
Dog, 177
Dragon, 150 f
Drink-offerings, 168
Dwelling-place of God, 137

EBED-JAHWE Songs, 26, 31 ff
— —, doctrinal teaching of, 85 ff
— —, reason for their presence, 35 ff.
— —, rhythm of, 88
Ecclesiasticus, 152
Edomites, 59
Efficacy of works denied, 120
Egypt, 7
—, emigration to, 51
—, Jewish colonists in, 8
Elisha's baldness, 162
Emendation of Hebrew text, 90
Emeth, 139
Endor, witch of, 175
Enoch, book of, 124 f
Esarhaddon, 7
Eschatological passages in Isaiah, 10, 12
Eternal life gained by alms, 119
Exegetical studies, 133 ff
Exiles, condition of, 55 f
—, intercourse with Judæa, 54
—, quality of, 51
—, returned, disillusionment of, 60
—, —, enemies of, 60
External influence on Jewish religion, 77
Externalism in worship, 62
Ezekiel, 46, 55
—, book of, 123
Ezra, 45, 62, 107, 111, 144
—, activity of after the Return, 114
—, followers of, 167
—, reforms of, 63
—, return to Jerusalem, 45

FASTING, spirit of, 109 f.
Forgiveness, 71, 74
Formalism, 43
Fusion of divine and human, 76, 82

GARDENS of Adonis, 172, 176
Gaumata, 61
Gedaliah, 53
Gehenna, 145
Gibeonites, 94
Gilboa, Mount, 174
Glory, the divine, 137
Gloss, explanatory, 151
Glosses, 16
God, apprehension of, 56, 104
—, conception of in later Judaism, 81

God, doctrine of, 74 ff
—, doctrine of in the Psalms, 74
—, false doctrine of, 103
—, majesty of, 56
—, quasi-personifications of, 127
—, relationship with, 104
Gods, national, 80
Goel, 139
Grace, divine, 73, 119
Great Rock, 141
Grecian period, 8, 49
Guardian angel, 127

HANANIAH, 54
Hand, 165
Headband, 161
Heathen customs, 62
— rites, 171
Heavenly hierarchy, 123
Hebrew text, emendations of, 90, 92, 114
— — corruption, 72, 88, 89 ff, 147
— word-play, 168
Hebron, 59
Hellenistic influences, 108
Heretical worship, 43
Hezekiah, Song of, 10
Hierarchy, heavenly, 123
Highway, 135
Historical background of xl–lxvi, 49 ff
— — of lvi–lxvi, 43 ff
"Holy," 179
Holy One of Israel, the, 77
Holy Spirit, 128
Hypocritical worship, 43

IDEALISM of Deutero-Isaiah, 29 ff
Idols, 79
Idumæa, 59
Imitations of Isaiah, 8
Incense altar, 173 f
Individual, the servant of the Lord, 85, 93
Infection, supernatural, 179
Isaac, 71
Isaiah, book of, apocalyptic passages in, 9
—, —, composite character of, 3
—, —, eschatological passages in, 10
—, —, historical references in, 3
—, —, non-Isaianic elements in, 5 ff.
—, style of, 15
— xl–lxvi, component parts of, 25 ff

JAHWE, a proper name, 27
Jeconiah, 54
Jehoiachin, 51, 52
Jehoiakim, 54
Jeremiah, 50, 55
Jerusalem, building of the walls of, 107
—, fall of, 55
—, Jews in after the Return, 58
—, reformation in, 62
— Talmud, 139

INDEX 183

Jewish colonists in Egypt, 8
— commentators, 123
— religion, external influence on, 77
Jews, advocate of, 127
—, distinguishing marks of, 56
— in Judæa during the Exile, 51
—, religious state after the Return, 153 f
John the Baptist, 134
Jordan, 59
Judæa a Babylonian province, 53
— after the fall of Jerusalem, 50 ff
— during the Captivity, 50 ff
Judaism, 44, 45, 63, 71, 75, 108, 118, 128, 129
—, background of early Christianity, 121
—, difference between Christianity and, 120
—, post-exilic, 121
Judicial murder, 98
Justification, 74, 119

KING of Jacob, 138

LAW, 12, 13, 44, 56, 120, 181, 144
—, new conception of, 107
—, observance of, 111 ff
Levites, 63
Life after death, 101
Logos, 126
Love, divine, 73

MAGIC, 178
Marginal notes, 16
Mark, 158
Marks, bodily, 162
Mattanah, 142
Mattaniah, 52
Mechiza, 137
Medes, 56, 61
Melek, 169
Memorial, 165
— after death, 152
Memorials in the house of God, 166
Memra, 128
Mercy, deeds of, 110 f
Merit, doctrine of, 119
Messiah, 86
—, advent of, 60
Messianic Era, 60, 112
— expectations, 61
— times, 17
Metatron, 128
Michael, 126
Midrash, 71, 86
Milkom, 170
Miriam, 142
Mixed marriages, 62
Mizpah, 53
Moses, 63, 125, 141, 142
Mourning, mark of, 162
Mouse, 177

NATIONAL gods, 80
Nebuchadrezzar, 50, 54
Nebuzaradan, 50
Nehemiah, 45, 63, 107 f
New views, beginning of, 67

OATH of fealty to the Deity, 166
Obliteration of sin by man's act, 72
— — — through suffering, 94
Old views, modification of, 67
Onkelos, Targum of, 141 f
Ordinances, legal, 113
Ownership, 158

PALESTINE, condition of, 58
—, excavations in, 169
Pargôd, 137
Parthians, 61
Particularistic views, 108
Paul, St , 141, 143
Peace, 96
Permanent and transient, 149
Persia, religion of, 57
Persian rule, 43
Personal responsibility, 56
Philistines, 59
Philo, quotation from, 126
Piggulim, 177
Plantings of Adonis, 171
Prognosticators, 163
Prophet, office of, 6
Prophet's badge, 160
—, *rôle* of, 122 f
Psalms, doctrine of God in, 74
Psammetichus, 7
Punishment for sin, 94
Punitive action, divine, 96

RABBIS, teaching of, 125
Rabbinical comment, 119
— literature, 126
Rahab, 150 f
Raphael, 125
Reckoning in O T , 50
Red Sea, passage of the, 150
Redeemer, 139
Redactional additions, 11 ff.
— —, reasons for, 19 f
— —, signs of, 20 f
— modifications, 11
Redactor, 11
Reformation in Jerusalem, 62
Relationship with God, 104
Religious state of Jews after the Return, 153 f
Responsibility, personal, 56
Rhythm in Ebed-Jahwe Songs, 88
Righteousness, 148
Rites, heathen, 171
Rock, 140, 143
—, spiritual, 141

SABBTAH, 56

Sabbath observance, pre- and post-exilic, 115 f
Sacramental symbols, 114
Sacrifice of dog, 178
Sacrifices, acception of, 69
—, animal, 101
—, non-necessity of, 72
—, spiritual, 103 f
Sacrificial system, 72
— —, abrogation of, 104
— —, cessation of, 114
— —, inadequacy of, 103
Samaria, 108
Samaritans, 58
Sargon, 7
Saul, 94
Scribes, 13, 18, 56
Seals, 158
Sennacherib, 7
Septuagint, 16, 21, 73, 98, 100, 134, 135, 137, 144, 148, 169
Servant of the Lord, 31 ff
— — —, characteristics of, 41
— — —, individuality of, 85, 93
— — —, Jewish belief concerning, 86
— — —, mission of, 40
Servitude, time of, 69
Shebaniah, 158
Shekhinah, 128
Sheol, 145, 170
Sheshbazzar, 57 f, 60
—, arrival of, 58
—, task of, 59
Sin involves suffering, 101
—, problem of, 56
—, punishment for, 94
Smooth stones, 168
Song of Hezekiah, 10
Sopherim, 56
Spartans, 177
Spiritual rock, 141
— sacrifices, 103 f
— suffering, 97, 101
Star-gazers, 163
Stigmata, 159
Suffering, 56
—, a means of atonement, 70
— a means of obliterating sin, 94
— an ethical necessity, 96
— not a sign of divine wrath, 102
—, spiritual, 97
—, the innocent for the guilty, 93 f.
—, voluntary, 94, 102
Superhuman beings, 121

Supernatural infection, 179
Superstitious beliefs, 180
Swine, 177
Symbolic act, 8
Symbols, sacramental, 114
Syria, 160

TAANACH, 174
Talmud, Jerusalem, 139
Targum of Onkelos, 141 f
— to the Prophets, 86
Tarshish, ships of, 18
Tattoo, 159
Tehom Rabbah, 150 f
Temple, 57
—, completion of, 61
—, foundation of, 57
—, rebuilding of, 60
— rebuilt, 44
—, the second, 61
Tetragrammaton, the, 26 f
Tiamat, 150
Tobit, book of, 125
Torah, 117
Transcendentalism, 74
Transient and permanent, 149
Tyre, lamentation over, 18

UNCLEANNESS, 179
Universalism, 8

VENGEANCE, divine, 94 f.
Ventriloquism, 175 f
Vicarious atonement, 101
Voluntary suffering, 94, 102
Vulgate, 135, 148

WATCHERS, 122 ff
Water and the Spirit, 138
Witch of Endor, 175
Wizards, 175
Word-play, Hebrew, 9, 168
Works, 74, 117 ff

ZECHARIAH, 162
—, book of, 123
Zedākāh, 119
Zedekiah, 52, 53
Zephaniah, 138
Zerubbabel, 60
—, Temple of, 61
Zodiac, stations of, 163

www.ingramcontent.com/pod-product-compliance
Lightning Source LLC
Chambersburg PA
CBHW071423160426
43195CB00013B/1782